WAR AND CONQUEST WITHOUT WEAPONS

Tactics and Strategies of Scorching the Phenomenon of Boko Haram in Nigeria

Published by

Adonis & Abbey Publishers Ltd

United Kingdom
Southbank House
Black Prince Road
London
SE1 7SJ
United Kingdom
Emails: editor@adonis-abbey.com,
Tel: 0845 388 7248

Nigeria
No.3 Akanu Ibiam Street,
Aso-villa, Asokoro.
P.O. Box 10546
Abuja
Tel: +234 (0) 8165970458, 07066997765

Year of Publication 2013

British Library Cataloguing-in-Publication Data
A catalogue record for this book is available from the British Library

ISBN: 9781909112346

WAR AND CONQUEST WITHOUT WEAPONS

Tactics and Strategies of Scorching the Phenomenon of Boko Haram in Nigeria

Otoabasi Akpan

Adonis & Abbey
Publishers Ltd

The costliest peace is cheaper than the cheapest war
– Sun Tzu

TABLE OF CONTENTS

CHAPTER ONE: Nigeria and its Security Dilemma

CHAPTER TWO: The Boko Haram Phenomenon

CHAPTER THREE

CHAPTER FOUR

Appendix A

BOXES

List of Abbreviations

BC	-	Before Christ
CIA	-	Central Intelligence Agency
DOD	-	Department of Defence (US)
DSS	-	Department of State Security
EXCOF	-	Executive Council of the Federation
FBI	-	Federal Bureau of Investigation
FDD	-	Federal Development District
GDP	-	Gross Domestic Product
GON	-	Government of Nigeria
GSM	-	General System for Mobile Communication
IC	-	Intelligence Community
IDPs	-	Internally Displaced Persons
JTF	-	Joint Task Force
LGA	-	Local Government Area
LGC	-	Local Government Council
LSG	-	Loss-of-strength Gradient
MASSOB	-	Movement for the Actualization of the Sovereign State of Biafra
MDAs	-	Ministries, Departments and Agencies
NAFDAC	-	National Agency for Food, Drug Administration and Control
NASS	-	National Assembly
NDLEA	-	National Drug Law Enforcement Agency
NIA	-	National Intelligence Agency
NODEF	-	Nigerian Overseas Development Fund
OPC	-	Odua Peoples' Congress
OPS	-	Organized Private Sector
SALWS	-	Small Arms and Light Weapons
SDD	-	State Development District
SFD	-	Special Federal District
SON	-	Standard Organization of Nigeria
SSS	-	State Security Service

SURE	-	Subsidy Re-Investment Empowerment Programme
SWF	-	Sovereign Wealth Fund
UN	-	United Nations
USA	-	United State of America
USSR	-	Union of Soviet Socialist Republic
VAT	-	Value Added Tax

Preface

This treatise is a product of petition and request from diverse sources, some of which include my post graduate students who feel that the Peace and Conflict Studies Programmes of the Department of History and International Studies of the University of Uyo should be useful and functional to Nigeria in particular and Africa in general by examining the different challenges of nation building and proffering workable solutions; Nigerians in diaspora who feel that Universities in Nigeria should take the lead in solving the myriads of problems facing Nigeria and lastly scholars in the field of Peace and Conflict Studies in the United Kingdom, the United States of America, Japan, South Africa and Ghana who, after reading three of my books, namely; *The Niger Delta Question and the Peace Plan, An Introduction to the Gulf of Guinea: People, History, Political Economy and Strategic Future and The Seven Practical Steps to Active Peace in Nigeria,* wondered why I should not beam the searchlight of my research on conflicts in Nigeria on the Boko Haram phenomenon which threatens Nigeria, the last hope of the black race.

Some of these scholars point to at least four Universities and two Think Tanks in Nigeria as active centres of scholarship in Peace and Conflict Studies and curiously my University is one of them. Altogether these "active centres" are; the University of Ibadan, Ibadan, Usmanu dan Fodio University, Sokoto, University of Jos, Jos, University of Uyo, Uyo; the National Institute for Policy and Strategic Studies (NIPSS), Kuru, Jos and the Institute of Peace and Conflict Studies, Abuja. The scholars are strongly of the opinion that researchers in the field of Peace and Conflict Studies in these institutions can bail Nigeria out through research and research findings.

This Monograph is produced largely to satisfy their curiosities and to underline the fact that Nigerian scholars can come out with ideas and prescriptions that can puzzle out the puzzles of the Nigerian state. Many of the institutions already mentioned have, over the years, done a lot to assist policy-and decision-makers in Nigeria to read the Nigerian barometer properly for effective governance. This Monograph from Uyo is just one of the many compasses available to the Nigerian state. It is hoped that it would stimulate thought-provoking ideas that would, together with other available documents, assist the nation tremendously.

In the course of writing this Monograph, I received support from many quarters and people too numerous to mention here individually. Notwithstanding their contributions, I am solely responsible for any defects in analysis or factual errors in presentation.

Otoabasi Akpan

Department of History and International Studies
University of Uyo
August, 2012.

Introduction

Boko Haram in Nigeria should be seen as both a phenomenon and as an activity. As a phenomenon it should be seen as expressions of injustice and de-development in Nigeria and as activity, it should be seen as expressions of violence and destruction to satisfy orgiastic aspirations, especially in the northern half of Nigeria. Again, as a phenomenon, the coverage of Boko Haram is the entire Nigeria and Nigeria in the diaspora and as activity, northern Nigeria has been turned into one boiling cauldron with fear being personalized, while insecurity lurks in the streets. Indeed, the sword of Damocles now hangs on every head, especially in the northern region.

The deadly scenario provokes soul-searching questions. Why is Nigeria enmeshed in deadly conflicts? What conditions fertilize social violence in societies? What were the warning signals or accumulation of combustible materials that were ignored? What conditions engender peace and security in a plural society? Are the violence entrepreneurs engaging Nigeria in conversation or are they determined to crack its history? Is Nigeria sitting on a keg of gunpowder? Are Nigerian youths dissatisfied with the political economy of Nigeria? Is the aggression of the Boko Haram a product of frustration, religious messianism or terrorism? How can the swords of Damocles in Nigeria be turned into ploughshares? And how can the phenomenon of Boko Haram in Nigeria and its activities in its Northern half be scorched?

In probing these questions and interrogating these broad areas of challenges, I have put forward a thesis on conflicts and crises in Nigeria and strategic pathways of conflict resolution and crisis management in a form of Monograph entitled; *War and Conquest Without Weapons: Tactics and Strategies of Containing the Boko Haram Phenomenon in Nigeria.* It is expected that the thesis would generate anti-thesis which would ultimately lead to synthesis. It is this synthesis that Nigeria needs to exorcise both the phenomenon and activities of Boko Haram from Nigeria. The thesis is distilled from a number of sources made up of fairly recent research and publications embarked upon by the author in the areas of conflict, peace, diplomatic, intelligence and general security studies, especially in Nigeria and the Gulf of Guinea.

The Monograph is divided into four parts; all variations of the same theme and none is mutually exclusive. Part I is entitled: *Nigeria and its Security Dilemma*. It treats the general causes of the crisis of post-coloniality in Nigeria, conflicts and crisis as facilitators of active peace and perfect security in Nigeria as well as selected sources of security challenges in the country. The focus of part II which is entitled: *The Boko Haram Phenomenon* is a perspective analysis on the personality of Boko Haram. Part III examines the various tactics and strategies of tackling the phenomenon of Boko Haram. Part IV summarizes and concludes the Essay.

CHAPTER ONE

Nigeria and its Security Dilemma

Explaining the Causes of the Crisis of Post Coloniality in Nigeria

Nigeria achieved independence in 1960 and like most forward-looking nations in the international system, it desired both active peace and perfect security in order to develop economically and strengthen the cycle of peace, security and development, but since independence, active peace has eluded Nigeria because it never really worked for it and on account of this, perfect security equally eluded her.

Many reasons can be adduced for the inertia. In the first place, at independence, Nigeria did not strive to develop rational-legal institutions to drive the process of development in the country. Power rested on individual politicians and not on national institutions and this led to brigandage politics which centred on nepotism, parochialism, and short-termism. Lack of credible political institutions meant that the military was the sole guardian of the nation. Between 1966 and 1999, Nigeria was in the throes of military influence. Within this long period, the military destroyed the federal system of government and the local government system that were bequeathed to the country at independence. The destruction of federalism and the local government system in Nigeria is the major cause of the underdevelopment of the country and the root of its crisis of post-coloniality. Without the practice of federalism, for instance, in a multi-national and multi-religious country like Nigeria, the country will never rise beyond average possibilities. Federalism has a number of strategic values. According to Gabriel A. Almond, G. Bingham Powell, Russell J. Dalton and Kaare Strom (2008:107):

> Federalism is commonly thought to have several advantages. In culturally divided societies, it may help protect ethnic, linguistic, or religious minorities, particularly if they are geographically concentrated. It may serve as a check on overly ambitious rulers and thus protect markets and citizen freedoms. Moreover, federalism may allow subunits (such as states) to experiment with different policy programmes. Governments may thus learn from the experiences of others. In addition, citizens may be free to "vote with their feet" and choose the policy environment that best fits their preferences.

With regards to grassroots administration, most African states, including Nigeria inherited local government structures from colonial rule. This was because majority of the imperial powers favoured Indirect Rule as a means of governance. After independence, the strength of local democracy declined precipitously (Thompson, 2010). In most cases, local government was replaced by local administration. Where the British administered the people of Nigeria, for instance, through Indirect Rule and had peace, today's Nigerian rulers administer through direct rule and have lost the peace. Issues such as education, health, road maintenance and the collection of taxes are seized from local government and are now overseen ineffectively by national and state administrators in their far-flung capital cities. On the consequences of the new trend, Alex Thompson (2010:114) notes:

> As a result, national rather than local initiatives came to dominate, while local communities had little influence over the policy making decisions that most affected them.

As a matter of fact, Nigeria is a country that does not have majority ethnic groups though many claim they belong to some but where one or two or a combination of three cannot overwhelm others in an environment of over four hundred groups, in all departments of national life, it is strange to talk about the ethnic composition of Nigeria in terms of majority-minority groups. All are indeed of minority groups, though of different sizes. Because these minority groups which are geographically concentrated are not protected by federalism and the local government system, deterioration of relations ensues and leads to series of programmed injustice; injustice in turn leads to conflicts, crisis and violence. Arguably, violence does not thrive in an environment of justice. The prevalence of violence in all corners of Nigeria shows the existence and   institutionalization of injustice. The response to the spate of injustice led to the emergence of social actors in the land. These are armed robbers, assassins, hostage takers, kidnappers, fundamentalists, anarchists and secessionists. Because the Nigerian state cannot provide them with security and protection, they strive to structure their own security and in the process create dissonance and insecurity in the land. What particularly worsens the situation is that the country is locked on to the contagion of conflict thesis where conflict hot spots are replicated throughout the country.

The spread of civil violence across a wide range of area can be likened to the spread of infectious diseases between human carriers (Braithwaite, 2010). Therefore, cases of armed robbery, kidnapping and bombing in one area are spread in the manner of infectious diseases between regions. It is worth noting that once a case of civil violence is allowed to succeed in one area and is not contained like a typical contagion disease, it has the propensity to spread with even devastating impact into new regions. For instance, the bombing exercises were phenomena that were prevalent in the Niger Delta region of Nigeria. Today, they are pronounced in the northern part of the country as well and until Nigeria positively puts an end to their occurrences, they would soon become Nigerian-wide cases with devastating consequences. When that time reaches, there would be nowhere to hide, particularly for the high and mighty who are very visible in the society.

Just as maggots are attracted by decaying meat and food, so are anarchists, fundamentalists and terrorists attracted by conflict hot spots and choke points. Nigeria has to watch out by doing the needful to tame conflict monsters that threaten its national interest. It has to be told that social actors are the most difficult enemies to fight because of their shadowy nature; nobody fights a shadow successfully.

Therefore, the Nigerian government should aspire to turn Nigerians, especially the youths from the path of destruction to the path of construction of the Nigerian system. Already, it is the nature of governance in Nigeria that creates social actors that challenge the authority of the state. Several reasons account for this. One of such reasons is gleaned from the observations of Samuel Huntington (1968:1) that: "the most important political distinction among countries concerns not their form of government but their degree of government". Two, weak states; "invite collective dissent and revolution" (Lichbach, 1995:68), while strong states, according to David Sobek (2010:269): "decrease the rebel's expectations of victory … since (sic) any rational rebel would avoid conflicts with strong states, all else being equal, as compared to weak states". Three, as Ted Gurr (1970:235) advises nations, "If dissident coercive control is substantially less than the regime coercive control in both scope and degree, dissidents are not likely to be able to organize and sustain an internal war". Four, as Sobek (2010:269) equally advises states: "when the demands on the government overwhelm the capacity of government, then civil violence is the outcome". Five, actions or inactions of the state affect how the ***potential*** for political violence becomes ***actual*** political violence (Gurr, 1970). Six, civil violence is most likely to occur in; "societies that rely on coercion to maintain order in lieu of providing adequate patterns of value-satisfying action" (Gurr, 1970:317). Seven, oil is generally regarded as the resource most directly associated with the weak state capacity and the "resource curse" (Akpan, 2011). Strengthening this argument, Indra de Soysa and Eric Neumayer (2007:202) forcefully emphasize that:

> … Dependence on natural resources weakens states…because natural resource abundance allows states to become rentier economies, with few incentives for the ruling elites to develop the broader economy as would rulers of natural-resource-poor economies that are forced to provide broad public goods in order to raise productivity. Natural resource abundance might induce leaders to foster corruption, patronage and rent-seeking behaviour rather than effectiveness, efficiency, and competence.

Taken together, it shows that since independence Nigeria has been installing governments and engaging in politics, but no government has ever exhibited any manner of strategic governance. Rather the different governments have been exhibiting features of imperial administration. Strategic governance is the capacity of a state to mobilize its tangible and intangible resources to achieve its set goals and fulfil its worldview, while imperial administration is the dictatorial control of people to fulfil the paternalistic instincts and foibles of the leadership. What would then constitute the country's set goals and worldview? These may be condensed into three broad concepts of security, development and Africa's leadership. The brigandage politics of the first, second, third and even fourth republics in Nigeria, the series of coups of the 1960s, 1970s, 1980s and 1990s, the civil war of the 1960s and 1970s, programmed state terrorism since the 1970s, unemployment and loss of jobs since 1960 and general economic de-empowerment of the citizens and lack of basic infrastructure for economic growth and development do not point towards security and development.

18

In terms of Africa's leadership, Africa is vulnerable and is in a seemingly perpetual state of instability and crisis because Nigeria is vulnerable and in a perennial state of instability and crisis. Nigeria's leadership of Africa fits the saying that *in the land of the blind, a one-eyed man is the king.* In a tormented continent like Africa, Nigeria uses, at least on paper, the trinity of large size, abundant natural resources and big population to advertise itself as giant. Yet, there is nothing to show for this giantism because over the years the government has not mobilized the country's resources to achieve a big power status which it has a capacity for. This state of affairs forces many students of comparative politics to accept the conclusions of Richard Dowden that Nigerians have not been governed all these years by governments; rather, they govern themselves through intricate links and connections. In his seminal book, *Africa: Altered States, Ordinary Miracles* (2009:441), he asserts:

> ...By any law of political or social sciences it (Nigeria) should have collapsed or disintegrated years ago. Indeed it has been described as a failed state that works ... How? It's a mystery. The secret lies in the layers of millions upon millions of networks, personal ties, family links, ethnic loyalties, school fraternities, church connections and scores of other unrecorded, informally organized bonds of trusts that make things happen. **Forget the government, the formal structures. What makes Nigeria work is a matrix of social, political and economic connections that ensure most people get food and shelter.** The hidden wiring also create Presidents, makes fortunes and prevents wars. But it also ensures that the vast majority of Nigerians are kept outside the ruler-owner circle, never given the chance to fulfil their – or Nigeria's potential.

This is a damning indictment of governance in Nigeria. In any case, these sad conditions occur because since the 1970s, the country's budgets have not depended on domestic revenues (like taxes or borrowing) and this has made the Nigerian state to be largely autonomous from the Nigerian society. Unlike serious states with principles of strategic governance that must bargain with social groups to generate revenue for public projects and to pick the bills of the state, rentier states like Nigeria can sustain themselves independently of social pressures and powerful interest groups. This is the tragedy of the Nigerian state. Undoubtedly, massive revenue from petroleum products is a major reason for the country's unresponsiveness to social demands, series of state terrorism and anarchy in governance. But these conditions need not persist. Nigeria has the capacity to retool and succeed brilliantly. On the impact of a successful Nigeria on Nigeria and Africa and the consequences of failure, Richard Dowden (2009:441) documents:

> A successful Nigeria could transform the continent (of Africa) in the twenty first century. Its resources grow more valuable as they become globally scarcer. Among the world's biggest oil producers; it is becoming one of America's main suppliers. Gas too has come on stream and production is expected to double and double again in the decade. It's 120 million plus people – or is it 140 million? The numbers are disputed like everything else in Nigeria – are a quarter of sub-Saharan Africa's population and among them are astonishing talents. In business, law, science, art, literature, music, sport, Nigeria produces phenomenally talented individuals as if its superheated society throws up brighter, hotter human beings than anywhere else. The leader who manages to harness and direct all that energy – physical and human – will create a formidable country that will change Africa and the world. Were it to implode like its neighbours, Sierra Leone, Liberia and Cote d'Ivoire, the human catastrophe would be unconscionable and it would take much of West Africa with it. Nigeria lives on edge.

It is a truism that Nigeria has the capacity to become a major power on the threshold of a superpower status within a decade of being led by resourceful and responsible leadership. Outside visionary leadership, the country cannot rise above average possibilities. In extreme cases, inept leadership would tip the scale and cause implosion. Unlike the Richard Dowden thesis that imploded Nigeria would "take much of West Africa with it", the simple truth is that imploded Nigeria would take the entire Gulf of Guinea with it. And this would be a tragedy not just for Africa but also for the Black World.

In order not to think the unthinkable and imagine the unimaginable, the Nigerian state should re-invent its national security and interest and at the same time re-configure its principles of state policy by way of political and economic restructuring in order to develop the country and give it a sense of direction. Nigeria may operate democracy as most countries in the Western World but if the democratic traditions are not deep enough, the country would not come out of its weak state status. This implies a continuation of the activities of social actors. Secondly, if the country does not rely on strong institutions as against strong politicians, then it would not go further enough in re-positioning itself for agents of economic development to thrive. Thirdly, if government remains the "only game in town" and built around oil without diversification of the economy, then the degree of vulnerability would continue to be high with no hope for development. In the final analysis, the perfect antidote to conflicts and violence is economic development. This position is supported by the World Bank Policy Research Report (2003:54) which states as follows:

> ... the key root cause of conflict is the failure of economic development. Countries with low, stagnant, and unequally distributed per capita incomes that have remained dependent on primary commodities for their exports face dangerously high risks of prolonged conflict. In the absence of economic development neither good political institutions, nor ethnic and religious homogeneity, nor high military spending provide significant defences against large-scale violence. Once a country has stumbled into conflict powerful forces – the conflict trap – tend to lock it into a syndrome of further conflict.

Nigeria depends primarily on oil for its exports and there is a terrible sense of unequal distribution of income. Apart from the oil producing regions that have been dastardly short changed and which is a major cause of conflict in the country, across the constitute states, there is lack of sufficient political will to redistribute income in order to absorb economic shocks. One credible way of doing this is to arrange the tax regimes so that the rich can take care of the poor, but this is not happening despite the fact that Nigeria is the most religious nation on earth and the two foremost monotheistic foreign religions of Christianity and Islam instruct the rich to care for the poor. Everywhere there is a huge gulf between the rich, who own several houses and cars, and the poor who barely have enough to eat.

In the northern part of the country which is the hottest bed of anarchism, there are millions of sleek cars that daily pass by the have-nots who merely beg to exist, yet these down trodden know too well the religious instructions that are not complied with and they know that owners of these vehicles do not pay taxes on the vehicles or tenement rates on their palatial palaces. In response, they torment the society and symbols of governments. In point of fact, majority of the people in the region may be illiterate in the sense of western education but are literate in the language of the Holy Book and they practically know that they are dealing with aspects of governmental oppressions. Muslim economics revolves around welfarism, equity and egalitarianism and any leader who neglects these principles must court anarchy and revolution. Oppression led to the Jihad of Usman dan Fodio in 1804 in the same region. During the reign of Mohammed Rumfa (1463–99) in Kano, Abd al-karim al-Majhili wrote; *The Obligations of Princes* as a handbook on statecraft for rulers in the region. The codes and instructions contained in the book are of immense value to the Nigerian leadership today. Without a good package of welfarism, northern Nigeria will never know peace and by implication, Nigeria will never know peace.

In the south, the same pattern of undeserved wealth is displayed and the nouveaux riche are not seen as being productive but products of clientelism and neo-patrimonialism. Therefore, the have-nots enter into the brotherhood of evil to torment the society and symbols of government.

Whereas in the north, a historical framework for responding to oppression has been a Jihad for which modern Nigerians of northern extraction are claiming to embark upon, in the south, it is insurgency which first began as a part of resistance to colonial rule. A continuation of oppressive colonial policies which express themselves in volumes of injustice in the south is implicated in many cases of violence in the region. Therefore, the central government should take a historical and sociological look at the causes of challenges to its authority in the country and it would discover that there is no religious crisis in Nigeria; just as there is no ethnicity in its politics. All problems are rooted in the politics of the economy and the economics of politics.

Nigeria must learn to know that governments are not run on natural resources but taxes. The advanced countries that Nigeria claims to emulate extract resources from taxation for development and for purposes of distribution of income. Sweden, for instance, extracts more than 50 percent of its GDP in taxes. The general trend, according to Gabriel Almond *et al* (2008:134) is that:

> The tax profiles of different countries vary both in their overall tax burdens and in their reliance on different types of taxes. Sweden has the highest tax rates overall, as it extracts more than 50 percent of its GDP in taxes. France comes close to the 50 percent mark. Britain and Germany are among a

number of advanced industrial societies that collect about 40 percent of GDP, while the United States and Russia extract about a third. Outside the European and North America areas, central government revenue rarely exceeds 20 percent of GDP. The central government revenue of India is under 15 percent or about 20 percent more if we add state and local governments.

On account of these realities in countries that are already developed, Otoabasi Akpan (2011:256) was forced to comment that:

The countries that we envy on account of giant strides in development have clear means of getting the rich to pay to assist the poor and they tax on conspicuous and ostentatious consumption like fuel, alcohol, tobacco, gambling and certain categories of property. In some countries, even the parking of vehicles in certain areas attracts taxes. Nigeria should not be an exception. Of what use is it for citizens to have exotic cars in excess of need and they are in most cases parked in the garages? This attitude constitutes great wastage to the economy and should be moderated through tax. In Europe, the average value of Value Added Tax (VAT) or Sales Tax is 18 percent; in West Africa it is 15 percent; in Greece it has just been increased from 19 percent to 23 percent; in Britain it has just been increased from 17.5 percent to 20 percent and in Nigeria it is only 5 percent. Economies are run on taxes but sadly in Nigeria it is run on petroleum resources. Yet Nigerians crave for development when they are not ready to pay for it. It is instructive to note that mankind has come into the world to perform seven duties namely; taxation, worship, sex, food, care for nature, sacrifice and to leave the world better than he found it. Nigeria should reform its tax system and profit there-from. Proceeds from taxes could achieve a lot in terms of economic development and employment which would in turn promote national development.

On why Nigeria should restructure its tax system to get the rich to care for the poor, the same author (2011:257) notes:

On the issue of taxation, Nigerians should be reminded that in African social organization, individuals do not enjoy absolute control over their wealth and the two foreign religions in which they are strong adherents reinforce the African tradition through the principles of **tithe** and **charity**. These imply the principles of sharing and what structure of sharing in modern times would be better than taxation. In point of fact, since the Nigerian independence, there has never been a single generation of Nigerians that have consciously borne the burden of the past, present and future generations of Nigerians. And without a generation sacrificing themselves, their leisure and all for the collective goal of all, Nigeria cannot develop. In the history of development of nations, one generation must stand out to impose a measure of sacrifice on themselves to move their nations forward so as to wipe out historical shame and humiliation they may have suffered in the past and to present the future generations with permanent platform for greatness. All advanced countries in the world are typical examples of this reality. Nigeria cannot pretend to be an exception if it seriously desires to develop. Without doubt, the first step towards the needful sacrifice is taxation. To this extent, evasion of tax and involuntary insurance schemes should attract the highest sanctions and penalties in the country; higher than murder, arson, armed robbery and assassination.

Inequality occasioned by improper distribution of income and inappropriate taxation is implicated in the continuous state of underdevelopment in Nigeria.

Finally, the greatest cause of crisis of post-coloniality in Nigeria is the fact that decision-makers, especially in the aftermath of the Nigerian Civil War, do not take decisions based on knowledge derived from research but on the emotions and preferences and even foibles of their political leaders. Universities, Research Institutes and Think Tanks are centres that should drive the nation and proffer solutions through research findings. All developed nations depend on these centres for guidance and direction but Nigeria depends on generalists, politicians and contractors for guidance. That the country would fail is inevitable. This is because, as Aristotle opined, "knowledge is the object of enquiry and man does not know anything until he discovers the why of it". An enquiry involves research and knowledge is distilled from research. Indeed, without research, there can never be development. The critical challenge of development in Nigeria is that the Think Tanks are few in existence while the Universities and Research Institutes exist in quantity and not in content and quality. To this extent, they are no longer temples of knowledge where all should worship and drink from their fountain. The implication is reflected in the quality of decision-making in the country and choice of policies. Beyond that, it is sad to note the pains that the country imposes on itself by relying on so-called foreign experts and foreign institutions who do not know anything about the country, its history, values and aspirations, yet propound elegant theories on how the country should go about taking care of itself. Michael P. Todaro and Stephen C. Smith (2004:125), call this approach to development the False-Paradigm Model. Writing on its content, they note:

24

A ... less radical international-dependence approach to development, which we might call the false-paradigm model, attributes under-development to faulty and inappropriate advice provided by well-meaning but often uninformed, biased, and ethnocentric international "expert" advisers from developed-countries assistance agencies and multinational donor organizations. These experts offer sophisticated concepts, elegant theoretical structures, and complete econometric models of development that often lead to inappropriate or incorrect policies.

Two of such expert advices are the Niger Delta Master Plan and Privatization Programmes. The documents on these projects which ordinarily should be thrown into the dustbin because of their inappropriateness are still used as guiding lights despite the fact that they are still counter-productive. The Niger Delta Master Plan, for instance, does not capture the essence of the problems of the people which in terms of age is 600 years old and the solutions proffered do not include environmental and fiscal justice, especially for the oil bearing communities. Conflicts and crisis in the region will not come to an end except these points are first captured and the country takes steps to withdraw from engaging itself in palliative measures and embrace active peace.

With regards to the privatization programme in the country, it is worth noting that it is a worthwhile venture but its operation, as advised by the Bretton Woods Institutions in a Third World country like Nigeria, is counter-productive and a trigger of conflict. Documenting the many mistakes in the policy and implementation of privatization programme in the Developing Countries, Joseph Stiglitz (2004:73), the winner of the Nobel Prize for Economics in 2001 and who was also the Chief Economist at the World Bank until 2000 writes:

Perhaps of all the IMF's blunders, it is the mistakes in sequencing and pacing, and the failure to be sensitive to the broader social context, that have received the most attention – forcing liberalization before safety nets were put in place, before there are an adequate regulatory framework, before the countries could withstand the adverse consequences of the sudden changes in market sentiment that are part and parcel of modern capitalism; forcing policies that led to job destruction before the essentials for job creation were in place; forcing privatization before there were adequate competition and regulatory frameworks. Many of the sequencing mistakes reflected fundamental misunderstandings of both economic and political processes, misunder-standings that were particularly associated with those who believed in market fundamentalism. They argued, for instance, that once private rights were established, all else would follow naturally – including the institutions and the kinds of legal structures that make market economies work.

Concluding on the fallout of lack of sequencing, he further records:

Even if Smith's invisible hand theory were relevant for advanced industrialized countries, the required conditions are not satisfied in developing countries. The market system requires clearly established property rights and the courts to enforce them; but often these are absent in developing countries. The market system requires competition and perfect information. But competition is limited and information is far from perfect – and well-functioning competitive market can't be established overnight. The theory says that an efficient market economy required that **all** of the assumptions be satisfied. **In some cases, reforms in one area, without accom-panying reforms in others, may actually make matters worse.** This is the issue of sequencing. Ideology ignores these matters; it says simply move as quickly to a market economy as you can. But economic theory and history show how disastrous it can be to ignore sequencing. The mistakes in trade, capital liberalization, and privatization described earlier represent sequencing errors on a grand scale.

Were Nigeria to rely on research from its Universities, Research Institutes or Think Tanks, a number of *residuals* unaccounted for by foreign experts would have been taken into consideration by Nigerian experts and these would have mitigated the disasters that the Niger Delta Peace Plan and the Nigerian Privatization Programmes are. These residuals include culture of the people, attitudes towards change, timing, sequencing and pacing.

Conflict and Crisis as Facilitators of Active Peace and Perfect Security in Nigeria

For Nigeria to develop, it has to come to terms with basic facts about conflicts and crisis. Conflict occurs as a result of incompatibility of interests and the interests of two or more parties must always clash. Therefore, conflict is inevitable and inexorable in the affairs of men. Several reasons account for this. One, the values and moral preferences of human groups differ from one another thus giving rise to conflict. Two, the inherited cultural values and practices of groups may differ so much between one group and another as to make a common mind on their mutual affairs difficult, if not impossible, to achieve. Three, the goals, ambitions, aspirations, intentions, wants, plans, desires and fears of individual human beings differ within the same society thereby resulting in the pursuit of incompatible interests that generate conflict and crisis.

Individuals and countries need not run away from conflicts because they must always occur but mankind needs to always create adjustment mechanisms to take care of conflicts once they occur or make adequate adjustments in interest so as to avoid occurrences of violent conflicts. Once adjustment mechanisms are in place, conflicts may not degenerate into crisis.

Though conflict and crisis are erroneously seen as synonyms they do not mean the same thing. While there may be conflict without a crisis, it is unthinkable to think of crisis without conflict (Akpan & Galadima, 2003). Therefore, crisis is but a stage in conflict. Crisis is a deciding moment or turning point in conflict. The hallmarks of crisis include, but are not limited to:

* Unanticipated surprise action by the opponent;
* Perception of great threat;
* Decline of open communication among disputants;
* Perception of limited time to make a decision or response;
* Lack of trust between disputants;
* Open and public verbal dispute;
* Breach of expectations by the parties involved; and
* The existence of physical aggression or fight between the parties.

For Shedrack Best (2009:110), a crisis is an

> Extreme situation of conflict which has reached turning point, where critical decisions have to be taken or else the conflict escalates to a point of extreme violence. Sometimes, a crisis is a degenerated state of conflict, where threats to human security, intense violence characterized by fighting, death, injury, large-scale displacement of populations occur.

Conflict has both constructive and destructive elements. Societies should always be ready to use it as a facilitator of active peace and perfect security. Acknowledging the creative nature of conflict, John Burton states:

> Conflict like sex, is an essential creative element in human relations. It is the means to change, the means by which our social values of welfare, security, justice and opportunities for personal development can be achieved. If suppressed ... society becomes static ... (Conflict is) neither to be deprecated nor feared ... indeed, conflict, like sex, is to be enjoyed.

By way of summary, a crisis occurs when decision-makers are:

1) Surprised by an event;
2) feel threatened (especially militarily); and
3) Believe that they have only a short time to react (Brecher & Wilkerfeld, 1997:21).

The more intense each of the factors is, the more acute the sense of crisis. But conflicts and crises are generators and guarantors of security and peace in societies that recognize their values and deliberately strive to use them functionally.

Fundamentally speaking, even when parties in conflicts see themselves as enemies, it is worth noting that enemies are strategic and important in life. Many writers (Simmel, 1955; Coser, 1968; Barash, 1994) place a premium on enmity. Simmel and Coser, for example, argue that groups may benefit from the existence of enemies, inasmuch as enemies provide something around which group members may rally (Tidwell, 2004). Barash (1994:10) goes even further to explore the value of enemies by arguing that:

> Enemies make history, not in the simple sense of producing important and noteworthy events, but in the deeper, literal sense of creating history itself. Without enmity, life – or at least, its political aspect – is deprived of meaning and literally seems to stop.

Tidwell (2004:127) emphasizes that: "By way of metaphor, enmity is the fuel that drives human social behaviour and experience". Coser on the other hand argues that: "rather than look at the existence of an enemy being pathological, it is best to understand the conditions under which enemies arise" (see Tidwell, 1998:128).

Therefore, the society needs enemies and/ or conflicts as guides for positive transformation. That is why A.F. Auckland (see Olagunju, 2002:27) asserts that conflicts, for instance, are not only inevitable, they are also positive and sometimes desirable to:

* Effect necessary changes;
* Generate new ideas;
* Test existing and novel ideas and the boundaries between the possible and the impossible;
* Reveal and exorcise fears;
* Build Teams;
* Reveal different needs and interests among individuals and groups;
* Explore personalities;
* Learn about each other;
* Enable people to express strong feelings;
* Discover the way other people think;
* Reveal or discuss fears about each other and about personal failure; and
* Create mutual dependence.

For Nigeria, the choice is clear: it has to set in motion the processes of achieving active peace and perfect security. The many conflicts and crises in the country involving the government and social actors should be used as facilitators of the much-desired active peace and perfect security. In trying to achieve these, the country should go about sorting its problems practically and not to rely on the current trial-and-error approach which has so far not worked for as John Burton and Frank Dukes (1990:20) argue:

> If one is lost in a forest, trial and error could be a useful procedure. But trial and error applied to dispute or conflict situations, in which the quality of life and life itself may be at stake, is unacceptable.

This Monograph attempts to guide Nigeria on how to structure out itself in order to save itself from itself and achieve active peace and perfect security. Active peace and perfect security are earned through deliberate efforts and not through trial-and-error nor can they be achieved through reliance on old techniques that have so far failed or are even absolutely obsolete and retrogressive.

One clear agent of development in the history of mankind, which is also an eternal guide, is *change*. Without change and its associates such as creativity and innovation, man cannot sustain his civilization and comfort. Portugal and Spain that in 1494, through the Papal Bull of Demarcation, divided the world into two for themselves; east for Portugal and west for Spain declined because of the neglect of the values of change, creativity and innovation. Other big powers that replaced them like Britain, France and Germany similarly degenerated because of neglect of this trinity of sustainable power and were overtaken by other power centres like the United States of America (USA) and the Union of Soviet Socialist Republic (USSR) (as superpowers) in the aftermath of the Second World War. By the 1990s, the USSR abandoned the political trinity and degenerated. Today, most European states are on the threshold of degeneration. Degeneration of countries occurs when they neglect the elements of modifiers of power. These are six in number and they are: quantity, availability, change, sustaining capacity, substitution capacity and qualitative differences (Jones, 1979).

Nigeria should weigh itself and find out whether it measures up to the power factors. What is the qualitative difference between Nigeria, that is seemingly not at war and Afghanistan and Iraq that recently came out of war? What is the quantity of its skill base in a world that is globalised and competitive? What is its level of sustaining capacity in the face of population explosion? Should the unimaginable occur in the oil industry- what is its strategy of substitution capacity? Answers to these questions make scholars to readily know why Ethiopia and Ghana lost their positions of Africa's leadership to Nigeria. The country has to watch out because it may have to lose that position to another country in the continent on account of steady neglect of modifiers of power.

Therefore, if Nigeria desires to progress and prosper, it has to hook itself up with modifiers of power and savour as well the competitive advantage factors of Professor Michael Porter (1991) of the Harvard Business School. These factors are:

1. Competitive advantage grows fundamentally out of improvement, innovation and change;
2. Competitive advantage involves the entire value system;
3. Competitive advantage is sustained only through relentless improvements; and
4. Sustaining advantage ultimately requires a global approach to strategy; that is, extending a nation's home-base advantages to the international system and arena.

National Security: Conceptual Analysis

Security is a term that is often abused especially by those acting in the name of the state. This is because there is always poor and vague understanding of security and this in turn has led to an equally poor and vague means of attaining it. Where the term is not well defined and boundaries properly established, states may turn out to become the greatest single threat to the security of their citizens. The vagueness of its concept forced Abdel-Uah Bennis (2008:136) to write:

> National Security is a vague term, yet it has become one of the most widely used and abused terms in modern politics. It has been used by national governments to justify external aggression and internal oppression. Robespierre, Napoleon, Kaiser Wilhelm, Joseph Stalin, Senator McCarthy, Milosevic, and Saddam Hussein (to name a few) have all justified purges, restraints on the freedom of speech, press and assembly, character assassination and, in some cases, even mass-murder, in the name of the "National Interest" and the "National Security". Most countries that have launched significant military actions abroad have claimed that their actions were dictated by the requirements of "national security". The USA used a threat to national security to justify its intervention in Nicaragua in the 80s, Iraq used it to justify its invasion of Kuwait in 1990 and the USA used it again in Afghanistan and Iraq more recently. The search for security is universal. Almost all countries, except for Costa Rica and Iceland, maintain military forces and commit up to 30% of total economic output (GNP) for arms, dedicated to maintain internal security and to stave off external threats. Governments maintain armed forces to deter or cope with crime, rebellions, secessions, coups and the possible threat, real or perceived, from other states or non-state actors such as terrorist groups, against the lives of their citizens, their private activities, against the territorial integrity of a country or its values and way of life.

For reasons of ambiguity, Barry Buzan (1983:4,9) points to:

> The hazards of a weakly conceptualized, ambiguously defined, but politically powerful concept like national security, which offers scope for power-maximizing strategies to political and military elites, because of the considerable leverage over domestic affairs which can be obtained by invoking it.

According to Tom Imobighe (1983:1):

> Security has to do with freedom from danger, fear, anxiety or uncertainty. It is a condition of being protected from, or not being exposed to, danger. A secure state is therefore one that is reasonably free from, or not being exposed to, external aggression or internal sabotage.

Speaking rather generally, there are various different ways that security can be conceptualized as Box 1.1 shows but the one that appears to capture the essence of it is that given by Barry Buzan, Ole Waever and de Wilde. According to them (1998:21), "security is about survival. It is when an issue is presented as posing an existential threat to a designated referent object (traditionally), but not necessarily the state, incorporating government, territory, and society".

The notion of survival expressed in the definition is apt because survival is central to the state of continuous livelihood or existence. Therefore, when a question mark hangs on the issue of survival of an entity or system, that entity or system is in danger of being phased out or destroyed or completely annihilated. States, governments and societies are known to be destroyed and annihilated by forces posing as existential threats to them. Security then could be taken to be the absence of existential threats to core values and modes of survival of an entity or system. In the final analysis, it is the capacity to turn hostility into cooperation, injustice into justice and challenges into harmonies (Akpan, 2010).

Box 1.1: Different Definitions of Security

Security itself is a relative freedom from war, coupled with a relatively high expectation that defeat will not be a consequence of any war that should occur.
Ian Bellamy, "Towards a theory of international security", Political Studies, 29/1 (1981:102)

Security-insecurity is defined in relation to vulnerabilities – both internal and external – that threaten or have the potential to bring down or weaken state structure, both territorial and institutional, and governing regimes.
Mohammed Ayoob, The Third World Security Predicament (Boulder: Lynne Rienner, 1995:9)

A nation is secure to the extent to which it is not in danger of having to sacrifice core values it if wishes to avoid war, and is able, if challenged, to maintain them by victory in such a war.
Walter Lippman, cited in Barry Buzan, People, States and Fear (Hemel Hempstead: Harvester Wheatsheaf, 1991:1).

Emancipation is the freeing of people (as individuals and groups) from the physical and human constraints which stop them carrying out what they would freely choose to do ... security and emancipation are two sides of the same coin. Emancipation, not power or order, produces true security. Emancipation, theore-tically, is security.
Ken Booth, "Security and Emancipation", Review of International Studies, 17/4 (October, 1991:319)

National security may be defined as the ability to withstand aggression from abroad.
Giacomo Luciani, "The economic content of security", Journal of Public Policy, 8/2 (1989:151)

If people, be they government ministers or private individuals, perceive an issue to threaten their lives in some way and respond politically to this, then that issue should be deemed to be a security issue.
Peter Hough, Understanding Global Security (London: Routledge, 2004:9)

A threat to national security is an action or sequence of events that (1) threatens drastically and over a relatively brief span of time to degrade the quality of life for the inhabitants of a state, or (2) threatens significantly to narrow the range of policy choices available to the government of a state or to private, nongovern-mental entities (persons, groups, corporations) within the state.
Richard H. Ullman, "Redefining Security", International Se-curity, 8/1 (1983:133).

Security ... implies both coercive means to check an aggressor and all manner of persuasion, bolstered by the prospect of mutually shared benefits, to transform hostility into coopera-tion.
Edward A. Kolodziej, Security and International Relations (Cambridge: Cambridge University Press, 2005:25).

Security, in any objective sense, measures the absence of threats to acquired values, in a subjective sense, the absence of fear that such values will be attacked.
Arnold Wolfers, Discord and Collaboration (Baltimore: Johns Hopkins University Press, 1962:150).

Source: *Alan Collins – Contemporary Security Studies. London: Oxford University Press, 2007:3*

The security-survival logic of Buzan, Waever and de Wilde is extended beyond military security, the traditional security engagement of most nations to encompass four other categories namely: environmental, economic, societal and political security. Indeed, for the Copenhagen School of Security which Buzan is a leading figure, five dimensions of security are always presented – military security as well as environmental, economic, societal and political security. Noting the features of the five dimensions of security, Barry Buzan (1990:2) explains:

> Military security concerns the two-level interplay of the armed offensive and defensive capabilities of states, and states' perception of each other's intentions. Political security concerns the organizational stability of states, system of government, and the ideologies that give them legitimacy. Economic security concerns access to the resources, finance and markets necessary to sustain acceptable levels of welfare and state power. Societal security concerns the sustainability, within acceptable conditional patterns of language, culture and religious and national identity and custom. Environmental security concerns the maintenance of the local and the planetary biosphere as the essential support system on which all other human enterprises depend.

From this standpoint, Buzan (1990:7), sees security issues as relating principally to the "pursuit of freedom from threat ... Its bottom-line is about survival, but it also reasonably includes a substantial range of concerns about the conditions of existence".

Indeed, with the end of the Cold War, the concept of security has come under serious scrutiny from scholars and practitioners alike. There is a gradual conceptual expansion of security to include "human security". The 1994 Human Development Report, which is one of the most far-reaching attempts to re-think security, defines human security as people's "safety from chronic threats and protection from sudden hurtful disruptions in patterns of daily life" (UNDP, 1994). Seven types of security were listed as components of human security. These are: economic security, food security, health security, environmental security, personal security, community security and political security.

It is worth noting that security is always a "hyphenated concept", especially in the contemporary period, and is "always tied to a particular referent object, to internal/external locations, to one or more sectors and to a particular way of thinking about politics" (Buzan & Hansen, 2009:10). Barry Buzan and Lene Hansen have, in the course of presenting and examining four questions that structure international security studies broadened our understanding of the issues to look for in security. The first question is whether to privilege the state as the referent object. Security is about constituting something that needs to be secured: the nation, the state, the individual, the ethnic group, the environment or the planet itself. Whether in the form of "national security", or later, as traditionalist "international security", the nation/state was the analytical and normative referent object. In this direction, it may be useful to ask whether securing the state was seen instrumentally as the best way of protecting other referent objects.

The second question is whether it is worth including internal as well as external threats. For the duo, since security is tied to discussions about state sovereignty (whether as something to be protected or criticized), it is also about placing threats in relation to territorial boundaries.

The third question is whether to expand security beyond the military sector and the use of force. The fact of the matter is that the Cold War period was overwhelmingly about the military (conventional and nuclear) capabilities of foes, friends and self for "national security" to become almost synonymous with military security. To be sure, other areas were considered but there was "the need to incorporate economic vigour, governmental stability, energy supplies, science and technology, food and natural resources". These were, however, to be incorporated because they impacted on 'the use, threat, and control of force', and thus on military security, not because they were to be considered security issues in their own right' (see Buzan & Hansen, 2009:12). In the final analysis, a more sectoral widening of security included societal, economic, environmental, health, development and gender.

The fourth question is whether to see security as inextricably tied to a dynamic of threats, dangers and urgency. The concept of national security as developed in the Western World saw threats as coming from hostile opponents which had to be confronted with a sense of urgency. For example, Herz was of the view that "security" had to do with "attacks, subjection, domination and – when pushed to the extreme – annihilation. This would lead groups to acquire more capabilities, in the process rendering their opponent insecure and thus compelling both sides to engage in a vicious circle of security and power accumulation" (Buzan & Hansen, 2007:12; Herz, 1950:157). This linkage of security to urgency and to extreme and radical defence measures was central as the debates over the expansion of the concept of security gained ground in the 1990s. Some scholars especially of the Copenhagen School argued that the concept of security could be expanded as long as referent objects, threats and dangers were constituted with this logic of urgency and extreme measures (Waever, 1995; Buzan et al, 1998).

In the final analysis, it is worth noting that nations do not face the same scale of threats and, therefore, the reference objects would not be uniform. Some countries are more threatened by their neighbours whereas others, most especially the Less Developed Countries, are mostly threatened by their citizens. To this extent, nations must carefully analyse the sources of their security challenges and then locate the referent objects that should be securitized and at the same time have legitimate claims to survival.

Selected Sources of Security Challenges in Nigeria

Nigeria at the moment faces about a dozen sources of security challenges. It is imperative that the nation understands the areas of security weaknesses that are very critical to its very survival, yet are taken for granted and treated in a carvaliar manner. The sources are

1) Poverty
2) Nature of Frontier
3) Trans-national Organized Crimes
4) Availability of Small Arms and Light Weapons (SALWs)
5) Fundamentalism
6) Anarchism and Serial Killing
7) Insurgency
8) Terrorism
9) Weak Intelligence
10) Weak State Syndrome
11) Democratic Insecurity and Dilemma and
12) Globalization blues.

These are by no means exhaustive but they represent the broad security challenges facing the nation. We shall attempt to examine only six of them in turns (for analysis of the dozen sources, see Akpan, 2012).

1. Poverty

Poverty is the foundation of insecurity dilemma in Nigeria and as Adam Smith, one of the architects of capitalism, once said: "No society can surely be flourishing and happy, of which by far the greater part of the numbers are poor and miserable" (cited in Todaro & Smith, 2004:195). More than three quarters of Nigerians are poor and miserable. These are reflected in short-life span, malnutrition, low literacy rate, unemployment and uncertain future. Millions suffer from conditions of absolute poverty and poverty trap.

Absolute poverty is a situation where a population or a section of a population is, at most, able to meet only its bare subsistence essentials of food, clothing, and shelter to maintain minimum levels of living. These type of people only live to occupy spaces and do not exist to be productive and move away from the state of poverty. Of course, they cannot move because the state has not arranged economic possibilities to accommodate them. As they are not accommodated, their conditions become worse and result in poverty trap. Poverty trap is a bad equilibrium for a family, community or nation, involving a vicious cycle in which poverty and underdevelopment breed more poverty and underdevelopment, often from one generation to another. A typical scenario is that the parents were plagued by absolute poverty and poverty trap and could not take care of the children, and they in turn, as though carrying out the *Will* of their parents remain in abject poverty. Sadly, they produce more children and by implication, one of their kind – more than the rich people. As these set of people will naturally want to live, they become willing tools in the hands of anarchist-oriented individuals. They cannot be blamed if they are used for the simple reason that they are trying to design their own security which unfortunately is diametrically opposed to the notion of national security as defined by the nation's securitizing actors. The bottom line of their actions is that he who is down needs fear no fall. Poverty-stricken people are down already and that explains why they dare security operatives in most cases. Besides, a nation that does not protect the poor who are numerous and anonymous cannot ever protect the rich who are few and visible. Without doubt, poverty is implicated in the many insurgencies that take place in Nigeria.

To reverse the trend which might soon build up and become irreversible, Nigeria should re-structure its current imperial administrative system and establish as quickly as it can a system of devolved government. To this extent, it should turn all Federal Constituencies into Federal Development Districts (FDDS), all Wards into State Development Districts (SDDs) and all frontier Local Government Areas into Special Federal Districts (SFDs).

The FDDs should be developed as growth poles, where as local administration, it should be funded by both the Federal government and the Constituent states in a ratio of 50 per cent each. For example, the Akwa Ibom State government may wish to allocate the sum of two billion Naira to each of its Federal Constituencies in a year. The Federal Government should similarly allocate 2 billion Naira; thus making a total of four billion for each FDD in Akwa Ibom State. The same principle should apply in the case of SDDs, where a Local Government Council should allocate a fixed sum which should be replicated by the state government. The SDDs should tackle local administrative and social challenges in the wards.

All frontier Local Government Areas in Nigeria (see Appendix A) should be turned into SFDs and treated as security communities (for details, see Akpan, 2011, 2012 a, 2012 b). These communities should host all defence establishments and security agencies. In other words, the presence of all military and para-military forces should be felt in SFDs. The SFDs will provide for Nigeria the outer-most defence bulwark against smugglers, oil bunkerers, trans-national criminals, human traffickers and gun runners whose activities cost Nigeria over two trillion Naira yearly in addition to series of collateral damages. The GON should provide an annual grant of at least ten billion Naira to each SFD for special developmental purposes; indeed, for capital budgets, security instruments and defence installations.

Meanwhile, all Local Government Areas should be treated as a separate tier of government in principles and in fact. They should be completely autonomous of State and Federal Governments. While the SFDs should provide the outermost defence bulwark against economic saboteurs in Nigeria, the Local Government Areas will provide the innermost defence against deviants. Sparks of insecurity dilemma are first generated at the grassroots levels. The current state of insecurity in Nigeria is a direct reflection of the state of its local government system.

Essentially, Nigeria borrowed the presidential system of government from the US because of the experience of America which is a plural society like Nigerian. It was envisaged that the system of executive presidency would inspire Nigerians to look up to the president as instrument of nation-building and oneness. But in imitating the US, Nigeria forgot to note that America has 87,000 governmental units made up of 1 central government, 50 states, 3,034 counties, 19,429 municipalities, 16,504 townships, 13,306 local school districts, and 35,052 special districts – each of which has some constitutional or statutory power to make policies – which it should have copied as well from the outset.

Nigeria cannot have peace and development with an amorphous system made up of 1 central government, 36 states and 774 Local Government Areas; all of which are in the imperial orbit of the central government. To reverse the trend in order to enjoy the US experience in theory and practice is the meaning of the FDDs, SDDs and SFDs which should be created and given a good dose of autonomy along with the Local Government system. Therefore, all federal Constituencies, LGAs, Wards (9555 in all) and frontier LGAs should resemble the American governmental units in theory and practice.

In the final analysis, any counter-insurgency strategy in Nigeria, and, indeed, the so-called counter-terrorism, must be based on economic development for once poverty is conquered, all else would be conquered. Economic development is the most strategic bulwark against insecurity as underlined by Robert McNamara (1986:22) and Maumoon Abdul Gaygoon (see Imobighe 2010:479). According to McNamara:

> Security is development and without development, there can be no security …development means economic, social and political progress. It means a reasonable standard of living and reasonableness in this context requires continual re-definition; what is reasonable in an earlier stage of development will become unreasonable at a later stage.

For Gayoon, the President of Maldives:

> Economic development… is the frontline of battle… Remove the debilitating effects on poverty and the first – the most important – battle will be won, and quite possibly the war. It will never be enough, or indeed

good enough, for the small states ... to be just well defended bastion of poverty.

For Nigeria, war on poverty means war on insecurity as war on insecurity would ultimately translate into peace and security. All in all, the weapons for these wars can only be manufactured from the resources of economic development. Yet, at the moment Nigeria is neck-deep in modernization as against economic growth which is the foundation of economic development itself. For Nigeria to institutionalize security and peace, it has to retool its political economy.

2. Nature of Frontier

Nigeria is bordered on the north by Niger, on the east by Chad and Cameroon, on the south by the Gulf of Guinea and on the west by Benin. Of the four countries that border Nigeria, only Benin has a semblance of political stability and absence of insurgent elements. The other three are conflict-prone zones with Chad having the highest index of risk occasioned by activities of rebels whose strategic areas of manoeuvre is the Greater Horn. According to L. J. M. Seymour (2010), the Greater Horn, at its broadest comprises; the states of Sudan (North and South), Eritrea, Djibouti, Ethiopia, Kenya, Uganda, the Central African Republic, Chad, Libya, Egypt, Somalia, Puntland, the de facto state of Somaliland, and the multiple insurgent movements that operate within and across the territories claimed by these actors.

It should be noted that in this region, governments routinely destabilize rivals as a way of gaining leverage and combating their own insurgencies. Indeed, most insurgents find willing support from governments in the region, locking the states of the Greater Horn in a vicious cycle of destabilization and proxy warfare. Any country having common frontier with any state of the Greater Horn ought to strengthen its security because insurgents and fleeing rebels from the region which is awash with SALWs constitute threats to these neighbours. Nigerians should, therefore, not be surprised that Borno state is an epicentre of the activities of Boko Haram. Borno state shares border with Chad, an actor in the Greater Horn's geo-politics of instability. The Greater Horn is full of insurgent and terrorist groups and Chadians are about the most militarized people in Central Africa.

Geo-strategically speaking, Borno state is a part of the Greater Horn of Africa.

Without doubt, the issue of porous border is partly a problem facing Nigeria in its north eastern flank and these are clearly cases of weak state capacity and contagion of conflict from the Greater Horn. Writing on how such problems challenge weak states, Richard Jackson (2007:152) argues:

> Due to their internal fragility, weak states also face a variety of external threats. Lacking the infrastructural or coercive capacity to resist outside interference, weak states are vulnerable to penetration and intervention by other states or groups ... A related external threat comes from the spill over or contagion of conflict and disorder from neighbouring regions. Lacking the necessary infrastructural capacity to effectively control their borders, weak states can often do little to prevent the massive influx of refugees, fleeing rebels, arms smuggling or actual fighting. Major external shocks like this can seriously threaten the stability of the weak state.

Nigeria has to be wary of the insecurity sparks from the Horn of Africa. If one considers Franz Fanon's metaphor that Africa is shaped like a gun, the Gulf of Guinea is the trigger while the Horn of Africa is the breech. Therefore, states of sub-Saharan Africa, including Nigeria, should programme their security strategies to insulate themselves from the *Horn gift,* which is a legacy of the Cold War. They should first save themselves from the elements of the tragedy of the Horn before they could collectively move to save the region from itself.

What compounds the problem of the nature of Nigeria's frontier is that international boundaries created two peoples in the frontiers; one group in Nigeria and the other ones in Benin, Cameroun, Chad and Niger. In Benin, the Fon make up 40 percent of the population and the next largest group is the Yoruba which are historically related with the Fon. Inside Cameroun, majority of the groups in Akwa Ibom, Cross River, Benue, Adamawa, and Borno states relate directly and many trace their ancestries to Cameroun. They cross the international borders as if they move from one state to another in Nigeria. The linguistic groups in Chad include millions of the Chado-Hamitic group, which is related to the Hausa spoken in Nigeria and there are many Kanuri and Fulani in Chad, just as they are in Nigeria. Concerning Niger Republic, the largest linguistic group is formed by the Hausa, whose language is also spoken in Nigeria. This pattern of ethnic composition constrained two Nigerien Presidents in 1972 and

1984 to lament thus about the prospect of their country's relations with Nigeria:

> Do not be surprised if we are swallowed up by Nigeria. Our national routes are directed through Nigeria, our cattle are exported to Nigeria and many of our people come from there. If we are swallowed up, it will not be as much your fault for leaving us alone as it is ours – President Diori Hamani, 1972.
> By the time Nigeria is sneezing (economically) we are already hospitalized – Kountche, 1984

Additionally, there is no state in West Africa and parts of Central Africa (Cameroon and CAR) that does not have a sizeable number of the Fulani who are also present in large numbers in Nigeria. These people move freely from one country to another. Movements by groups in Africa should be encouraged but the people and their activities should be constantly monitored for security checks, evaluation and policy-making.

Nigeria has an extensive coastline in the Gulf of Guinea covering several kilometres. This poses a formidable security challenge to the country. The entire Gulf of Guinea has about 5500 kilometre-long coastline fed by the Congo, Ogoone and Niger Rivers, other numerous waterways and Creeks and the Bights of Benin and Biafra. Together these resources provide havens for criminals, especially those of the trans-national organized crime category. Criminal activities in the Gulf of Guinea are worth more than $100 billion a year. Such crimes include oil bunkering, narcotics smuggling, smuggling of precious metals and other natural resources, arms trafficking, human trafficking, sea piracy and illegal fishing. Already the Gulf's coastline is the second most violent coastline in the world after Somalia's coastline (Bakut, 2010).

Nigeria as a visible state in the Gulf of Guinea cannot be immune to the security torments that the Gulf of Guinea presents and what is more most of the states in the region are facing some degrees of insurgencies and challenges to their authorities.

Essentially, Nigeria faces serious security threats from its land and sea borders. The country has extensive international border of about 4900 kilometres made up of 773 kilometres with the Republic of Benin in the West, 1497 kilometres with the Republic of Niger in the North, 87 kilometres with the Republic of Chad in the North-West and

1690 kilometres with the Republic of Cameroun in the East and 853 kilometres of Coastline. On this score, Nigeria can only upgrade its security profile by re-thinking the concept of security away from the old stereotypes. This calls for the creation of at least four technified security outfits; the National Guard (NG), the Border Guards (BG), the Air Marshal and the Coast Guards (CG) to work in league with the Army, the Navy, the Airforce, the Immigration and the Customs Services. As Otoabasi Akpan has emphasised (2012:236):

> Nigeria should establish and equip special security forces to tackle special security challenges. Three of such special security forces are the Air Marshals (from the Air force), Border Guards (from the Army) and Coast Guards (from the Navy). Section 214 of the 1999 Constitution gives the NASS power to establish such security agencies. Sub-section C of the Section reads:
> The National Assembly may make provisions for branches of the Nigeria Police Force forming part of the armed forces of the Federation or for the protection of harbours, waterways, railways and airfields.
> While National Guards should take care of railways across Nigeria, including sensitive and strategic centres, environments and installations, Air Marshals should have a special mandate to take care of the security needs of the aviation industry – the airports and the airlines. Even though Nigeria does not experience terrorism, especially the types that involve hijacking and bombing of planes, it does not have to wait for tragedy to occur in the aviation industry before it acts. The phenomenon of terrorism in the aviation industry will take Nigeria back for more than fifty years, thus wiping the modest gains that the country has had since independence.

> On account of the porous waterways and borders with neighbouring countries, there is dire need for Border and Coast Guards to police these frontiers. To be sure, there are security establishments like the Navy, Customs and Immigration Services that are supposed to tackle security challenges from these frontiers but they are not enough and adequately tuned to tackle these peculiar challenges. The Navy, for instance, is a branch of the army which is most suited for war purposes and not for peace-time security challenges posed by non-combatant criminals. The Customs and Immigration Services are ill-suited to contain transnational organized crimes. There is certainly need for inter-agency relations, coordination and sharing of intelligence for effective security purposes but the security challenges posed by the air, water and land frontiers require special forces trained and equipped for the peculiarities of these challenges. Besides, these agencies should be well-trained in counter-insurgency and counter-terrorism techniques and above all should be skilled in intelligence and counter-intelligence measures.

These agencies should be well equipped with modern security instruments which incidentally abound in quantity and quality in technology supermarkets. Take the case of South Africa as example. The Republic has radar Surveillance installation which can monitor shipping throughout the Southern Oceans (Bowman, 1985; Akpan, 2000). Indeed, South Africa has the capacity to chart ship movement "in an operational arc ranging from the Antarctic to North America and from South America to Bangladesh" (Bowman, 1985:128). Nigeria should dominate the Gulf of Guinea with such technology and installations.

Domestically still, Nigeria should create SFDs as a matter of urgency. Internationally, progress can only be assured if the states of West Africa and the Gulf of Guinea unite behind stronger, more effective multilateral organizations.

3. Availability of Small Arms and Light Weapons

In UN parlance, small arms refers to pistols, rifles and carbines, sub-machine guns, assault rifles and light machine-guns; while light weapons (a separate category) refers to heavy machine-guns, grenade launchers, portable anti-aircraft guns, portable anti-tank guns, portable missile launchers, mortars of less than 100mm; and "ammunition and explosives" including cartridges for small arms, shells and missiles for light weapons, hand grenades, landmines, and explosives (see the UN General Assembly Report of the Panel of Governmental Experts on Small Arms: 11 – 12). These are all weapons of terror.

The world has in excess of 1 trillion SALWs and Africa has in excess of 100 million of these weapons (Akpan, 2007). According to the UN, only 3 percent of these arms are used by governments, military or paramilitary forces (Naim, 2003); the rest are in illegal hands especially in conflict-prone areas. Outside outright sales and military programmes, SALWs are spread through covert and "gray market" channels especially in Africa (Akpan, 2007). Their low cost nature, portability, ease of maintenance and operations make them perfect instruments for use by insurgents, criminal bands, separatist groups and other sub-and non-state actors (Jayantha, 2005). In fact, the increasing sophistication and lethality of some of these weapons have

44

given these social actors a firepower that often exceed that of any nation's security operatives.

With such weapons capable of firing up to 300 rounds a minute, one individual can threaten a society in no small measures. Besides, the simple nature of SALWs can be demonstrated with the use of AK 47. The assault rifle has about 30 moving parts and is so simple that it can be used and maintained by teenagers. Most of these weapons require few hours of training for users to be highly skilled in using them. That is why they are perfect partners of insurgents, criminal gangs, warlords and militia.

Nigeria must upgrade its treason laws to include possessors of unlicensed guns and ammunitions who should be classified as treasonists. In fact, for the country SALWs should be seen as Weapons of Mass Destruction (WMD) and categorized as such. Therefore, holders of unlicensed guns should be treated as treasonists; those who declare war on the nation. Beyond this, the country's law should be changed to reflect new realities; those in possession of illegal and unlicensed guns should be adjudged guilty already until they prove their innocence in a competent court of law. The same condition should apply to those who kill by guns regardless of intention and the establishments they represent except in war situations.

4.Weak Intelligence

Intelligence is a part of the "nerves of government" (Deutch, 1963). It is equally a part of the power of information rooted in the belief that to be forewarned is to be forearmed. Intelligence is the key to national security of nations but the problem as observed by James Der Derian is that like security itself, it is the "least understood and most *under-theorized* area of international relations" (1992:15).

There are many ways that intelligence is conceptualized and a few merits documentation. Thomas F. Troy defines intelligence simply as "knowledge of the enemy" (Troy, 1992:433). *The Economist of London* which is a respected periodical defines it as:

> The painstaking collection and analysis of fact, the exercise of judgement, and clear and quick presentation. It is not simply what serious journalists would do if they had time; it is something more rigorous, continuous, and above all operational ... that is to say related to something that somebody wants to do or may be forced to do (see Johnson & Writz, 2008:2).

Kent Sherman, an early theorist and practitioner of intelligence, defines it as knowledge, as organization and as an activity (Johnson & Writz, 2008). From this definition is a description of how intelligence services collect and analyze information, the finished intelligence product that agencies provide to policy-makers and the way intelligence services are organized (Kent, 1949). Providing a succinct description of the three facets of intelligence, Mark Lowenthal (2006:9), another intelligence theorist and practitioner, writes:

Intelligence as process: Intelligence can be thought of as the means by which certain types of information are required and requested, collected, analyzed, and disseminated, and as the way in which certain types of covert action are conceived and conducted.

Intelligence as product: Intelligence can be thought of as the product of these processes, that is, as the analyses and intelligence operations themselves.

Intelligence as organization: Intelligence can be thought of as the units that carry out its various functions.

Stan A. Taylor (2007:250) argues that intelligence:

Refers to the collection, analysis, production and utilization of information about potentially hostile states. It differs from other sources of information in that it is often, but not always, collected clandestinely and that states attempt to keep other states from obtaining it. It may include special activities meant to influence the foreign or domestic policy choices of other states without revealing the source of influence. Intelligence also refers to the government entities that collect and analyze information as well as to the process by which this function is performed.

A British academic, Ken Robertson has forcefully argued that:

A satisfactory definition of intelligence ought to make reference to the following: threats, states, secrecy, collection, analysis, and purpose. The most important of these is threat, since without threats there would be no need for intelligence services ... A threat is not simply an unknown factor which may affect one's interests but is something capable of causing serious harm or injury ... (Intelligence's) unique element is secrecy – the secret collection of someone else's secret (Robertson, 1987:46).

Secrecy is holiness in the world of intelligence. That is why Michael Herman emphasizes that: "Intelligence uses all types of information but is geared essentially to penetrating those areas in which concealment and deception are endemic" (Herman, 1989:28). On this score, Shulsky underlines that: "Fundamentally, intelligence seeks access to information some other party is trying to deny" (see Herman, 2008:118). In this business:

> The task of the intelligence officer is to tell the policy-maker what has happened throughout the world in the recent past, what is happening currently (and why), and what the future is likely to hold (see Barnds, 1975:13).

That is why the American CIA defines intelligence dryly as "knowledge and foreknowledge of the world around us – the prelude to Presidential decision and action" (CIA, 1983:17). Overall, this task is at times cloudy and a part of the Donald Rumsfeld **unknown unknowns** thesis (see Ayad, 2006: xiii). Speaking on the failure of intelligence on the 9/11 attacks on the US, he noted:

> There are things we know we know.
> We also know
> There are known unknown.
> That is to say
> We know there are some things
> We do not know
> But there are also unknown unknowns
> The ones we don't know
> We don't know ...

Since knowledge is power, a nation "needs accurate political, economic, and military intelligence regarding its rivals, its competitors, its enemies, and-yes-even its friends" (see Herman, 2008:115).

Power is only vested in those who filter information well. But the trouble is that: "the hard news and the hard information often comes later, the rumours come in first, often uncorroborated, the first draft; they are incomplete, inaccurate, and therefore unreliable ... The trouble is the new information technology is producing the rumours in this age when we're struggling to get on the information edge. It is these rumours which are making the impact…(Gowing, 2006:14). The fact of the matter is that members of the intelligence community have to deal with the challenges of the F3 acronym of being the *first* to know; getting the information *fast* and being confronted with the *flaws*. To get over the problem and cause information to become *power*, information must first be converted to knowledge and then to power through the following means and stages:

* Contextualization; which includes answering the critical questions why, when, where and how. The answers to these questions put vast amounts of data in their right context.
* Data-Mining; which consists of deriving useful information from a vast amount of data, and
* Condensation; which involves summarizing the vast amounts of information, without sacrificing the meaning (Bennis, 2006:133).

Information is not power; knowledge is power. Intelligence in the final analysis is information that has been processed into an instrument and or tool for the in-depth analysis of a given situation. It is the means used by governments to protect, guarantee, sustain and further their national interest.

Intelligence gathering, as an activity and an art, is commonly referred to as espionage or spying and it has followed human history. Espionage is as old as interaction between clans, tribes and societies. It is derived from the need to know! It is driven by curiosity about "the other" and their ways of life, their achievements, their strengths and weaknesses. Aspects of "intelligence" gathering have even been detected in the animal kingdom amongst animals such as otters, owls and monkeys (Bennis, 2006). Human history is filled with records of intelligence-gathering. The first records of human espionage activities date back to the ancient Japanese Feudal Empire. The masters of deception, the Ninjas, were used extensively in a game of spying and assassination, on behalf of their Masters, in preparation for war or negotiations. In one of the earliest records of uses of spies, Moses ordered spies into Canaan to 'spy out the land' to see whether or not the Israelites could occupy it.

The Chinese general Sun Tzu (ca 500 BC) devoted the last chapter in his widely read book, ***The Art of War***, to the role of spies. Sun Tzu, like most early users of intelligence, sought information about the military capabilities and plans of potential enemies. Ancient Rome also used spies to "keep an eye" on its neighbouring clans such as the Aequi, the Volschi and the Etruscans. Around 300 BC, during the Etruscan wars, Consul Fabius Maximus sent his brother disguised as an Etruscan peasant into the Crimean forests in an attempt to win the Umbrians over to the cause of Rome. Roman armies under Caesar scouted the movements and capabilities of enemy troops. Moslem armies used spies in their holy wars to spread Islam. As a result of the utility of espionage, Byzantium which was surrounded by scores of vigorous, blood thirsty and adventurous barbarian groups on its borders was able to survive for eleven centuries. Intelligence gathering was a key feature of the Byzantium diplomacy.

In pre-colonial Africa, the fame and military exploits of Dahomey were attained and sustained by ***Agbadjigbeto***, the kingdom's intelligence service, which was instituted by Agaja, its warrior-king. The service made Dahomey to survive series of epic battles and diplomatic intrigues. In pre-colonial Ibibioland in particular and the Cross River region in general, ***nsibidi***, the sign writing and language had complex intelligence value which stabilized the entire region and enhanced inter-group relations.

In the contemporary modern period, most large and globally active nations have some or all of the following types of intelligence agencies:

1. An overall supervisory office or group of offices charged with coordinating the several different agencies that make up a country's intelligence community (IC);
2. An agency responsible for collecting, analyzing, and producing intelligence drawn from foreign countries and other external sources;
3. An agency responsible for collecting, analyzing, and producing intelligence about domestic threats to security;
4. An agency responsible for the collection and distribution of signals intelligence (sigint);

5. An agency that works under the direction of the military department or departments of a government to provide intelligence required by military forces and;

6. Depending on size and global involvement, nations may have agencies specifically charged with anti-terrorism; the development, operation, and exploi-tation of satellite and overhead imagery; counterintelligence; border protection; and other special functions.

The nature of each agency varies according to the different political cultures, legal systems, and bureaucratic styles of each country (Taylor, 2007).

The United Kingdom (UK) has the Secret Intelligence Service (M16) as its foreign intelligence arm and the Security Service (M15) as the domestic intelligence; the US has the Central Intelligence Agency (CIA) as its foreign intelligence and the Federal Bureau of Investigation (FBI) as the domestic intelligence; Russia has the Foreign Intelligence Service (SVR) as its foreign intelligence and the Federal Security Service (FSB) as its domestic intelligence; France has the General Directorate for External Security (DGSE) as its foreign intelligence and the General Intelligence (RG) as its domestic intelligence; and Germany has the Federal Intelligence Service (BND) as its foreign intelligence and the Federal Office for the Protection of the Constitution (BFV) as its domestic intelligence.

Most of these services have to be very efficient in order to guarantee the national security of these states. Even a small country like Israel has a clinically efficient intelligence service, the Mossad. That is why though the state of Israel is almost surrounded by Arab states and she is located in one of the most tortuous environments on earth, she could contain series of security challenges on account of the efficiency of the Mossad.

Nigeria, like most states, has both foreign and domestic intelligence; the National Intelligence Agency (NIA) and the Department of State Security (DSS) otherwise called the State Security Service (SSS) respectively. Since intelligence organizations and operations are shrouded in secrecy, one may not know the extent of their man-power and resources to rate their operational performance; but since results are almost seen in form of security outcomes, then a huge question mark hangs on the efficiency of the country's IC. A country with an efficient IC would certainly not experience the scale of security dilemma or most appropriately the spiral of insecurity that Nigeria faces.

A way out of the problem is for Nigeria to restructure its whole paraphernalia of security and give pride of place to the IC. The foremost and most versatile member of the Nigerian IC, which is the SSS, should make good use of undercover agents in different professions like teachers, medics and mechanic(s) and ordinary citizens like students and traders in all Wards in Nigeria. Same with the Police. This approach requires great funding. Commenting generally, on how modern intelligence requires a financial war-chest and the consequences of the cost, Michael Herman (1995:2) notes:

> Organized intelligence ... has been a twentieth–century growth industry, and most governments now have it as a permanent institution. It is a significant part of the modern state and a factor in government's success and failure. It consumes sizeable if not massive resources; US expenditure on it at the end of the Cold War was about a tenth of the cost of defence, and the current British effort costs rather more than diplomacy. It has even had some direct economic effects, as in its influence on early computers and subsequently on the development of space satellites and miniaturized electronics. It constitutes its own particular kind of state power: **intelligence power**.

Besides, like in the case of the American CIA, the SSS should profit from the services of Ph.D. holders in the University system, Research Institutes and Think Tanks in all areas of specializations especially in its intelligence analysis. The Intelligence Directorate of CIA is much like an expanded set of University "area of studies" faculties. Commenting astringently on this, Turner writes:

> The analytical branch of the CIA is given to tweedy, pipe-smoking intellectuals who work much as if they were doing research back in the universities whence many of them came. It probably has more Ph.Ds. than any other area of government and more than many colleges. Their expertise ranges from anthropology to zoology ... (see Herman, 2008:119).

On account of this resourcefulness, breadth is a special characteristic of US intelligence. On this feature, R. M. Gates wrote in 1987 that:

51

The range of issues (studied) is breath-taking-from strategic weapons to food supplies, epidemiology to space, water and climate to Third World political instability, mineral and energy resources to internal finances, Soviet laser weapons to remote tribal demographics, chemical and biological weapons proliferation to commodity supplies ... (see Herman 2008:118).

Ph.D. holders who have passed through the crucible of scholarship – not those who ambush the degree from some backyard institutions – have immense capacities to puzzle out puzzles. Therefore, Nigeria should take a cue from clinical efficient ICs in other lands and become great; away from the current state of full decline.

Apart from the SSS, all military and paramilitary forces should have effective intelligence units. Effective and efficient intelligence can save the country billions of dollars that would otherwise be wasted by attacks on, and destruc-tions of, lives and property. A country with effective intelligence cannot be menaced successfully by domestic insurgents, anarchists and terrorists. The state of Israel is one such country.

Israel is a typical and sterling example of a country that cannot be menaced successfully by domestic and external actors. As an island of Christianity surrounded by seas of Islam and located in the most tortuous environment on earth, Israel, through its IC, the Mossad and its Defence Force, has insulated itself satisfactorily from security torments and spirals of insecurity in the Middle East.

The history of the Jews shapes beliefs for the modern state of Israel and makes it invulnerable on all fronts. The constant oppression experienced by Jewish people "reinforces the belief today that the paramount role of the state of Israel is to provide physical security for the Jewish people, who, for the first time since the Roman conquest of Jerusalem in 70CE, have their own state and their own security apparatus" (Sorenson, 2008:3). Between 1948 and 2009 the state of Israel fought ten external wars with their neighbours and defeated them all.

Domestically, the level of human security for the citizens of the state of Israel is so sumptuous that no citizen would want to form a brotherhood of evil to fight internal wars in the country. Though in size it is not up to the size of Cross River State of Nigeria and half of the country is located in the Negev desert, the average Israeli enjoys a standard of living comparable to that of most Western European countries, with a GDP per capita in excess of $30,000, which is the highest in the Middle East, outside the Gulf Emirates. The inflation rate is 2 percent and unemployment is 8.5 percent.

The country's status as an advanced economy can be gleaned from the fact that about 70 percent of its activity comes from the service sector – tourism, financial and health care – while industry is less than 30 percent and agriculture is less than 3 percent. About 30 percent of Israel's GDP comes from foreign trade as the economy is exported oriented. Even on its rocky terrains and landscapes, top soils are imported from Africa and Europe and covered on them to grow fruits for export. This is a serious attempt to achieve active peace. Israel earns about $100 billion a year from its exports.

The example of the state of Israel shows that national security is a combination of the main components of human and physical security; one of them cannot ever secure a country. Secondly, it shows that active peace that it (Israel) enjoys in a turbulent environment is a product of deliberate efforts and hard work (see Levite, 1987; Maoz, 2006).

The lesson for Nigeria is clear: something is either wrong with the Blackman, which Nigeria largely symbolizes, or with the system it operates. Without much ado, something is fundamentally wrong with the system that Nigeria operates. Imperial administration and politics in a plural society like Nigeria cannot ever lift the people up from the morass of insecurity.

For Nigeria to rise up to the security challenges facing it effectively, the component units like states and LGCs must be empowered to confront economic and insecurity dilemmas through the instrumentality of federalism. Imagining sly, Nigeria can contain a total of 46 states of Israel, each with a population of 8 million, mountain ranges and rocky soils. If Nigeria is so blessed by nature with clement weather, luxuriant vegetation, fertile soils, abundant maritime properties, large size; low population per state; but large national population, arrays of solid, liquid and gaseous minerals and a resourceful people and cannot achieve a big power status by its magic year of 2020, it should rent itself out to either a state or non-state actor to show it how it can turn it into a modern superpower within a decade. The continuous state of insecurity in Nigeria is simply unacceptable and its state of full decline in the midst of potentials for greatness should by now reach the limits of tolerance.

Like the domestic intelligence service of Germany, the DSS mandate should include the protection of the Nigerian Constitution as well. It should also monitor the activities of the police system in Nigeria.

Finally, the scope of Nigeria's IC should be expanded considerably. All military and Para-military agencies and sensitive MDAs should have intelligence units and should belong to the country's IC. In the US, apart from the CIA, the American IC is made up of about thirteen agencies (see Box 1.2).

Box 1.2: US Intelligence Community

Members of the U.S Intelligence Community

- Office of the Director of General Intelligence, which includes the Office of the Deputy Director of Central Intelligence for Community Management, the Community Management Staff, the Terrorism Threat Integration Centre, the National Intelligence Council, and other community offices
- The Central Intelligence Agency (CIA), which performs human source collection, all-source analysis, and advanced science and technology

National Intelligence Agencies

- National Security Agency (NSA), which performs signals collection and analysis
- National Geospatial-Intelligence Agency (NGA), which performs imagery collection and analysis
- National Reconnaissance Office (NRO), which develops, acquires, and launches space systems for intelligence collection
- Other national reconnaissance programs.

Departmental Intelligence Agencies

- Defence Intelligence Agency (DIA) of the Department of Defence
- Intelligence entities of the Army, Navy, Air Force, and Marines
- Bureau of Intelligence and Research (INR) of the Department of State
- Office of Terrorism and Finance Intelligence of the Department of Treasury
- Office of Intelligence and the Counterterrorism and Counterintelligence Divisions of the Federal Bureau of Investigation of the Department of Justice
- Office of Intelligence of the Department of Energy
- Directorate of Information Analysis and Infrastructure Protection (IAIP) and

Directorate of Coast Guard Intelligence of the Department of Homeland Security.

Source: *Johnson, L. K & J. J. Wirtz. 2008. Intelligence and National Security: The Secret World of Spies. Oxford: Oxford University Press: 441.*

From the box, it can be observed that the popular FBI (Federal Bureau of Investigation) in the US is a Departmental Intelligence Agency that belongs to the Department of Justice – equivalent of Nigeria's Ministry of Justice. From the American example, Nigeria can upgrade, for instance, its Code of Conduct Bureau and the EFCC to become members of the country's IC, where the former can keep a tap on, and or monitor, the conduct of all public servants and political officers across the three tiers of government, while the latter can double-check the activities of the institutions that make use of public monies across Nigeria. This way, corruption would be put at bay, while overall productivity in the country would be enhanced.

The Code of Conduct Bureau may be made an arm of the Ministry of Justice, while the EFCC should be attached to either the Central Bank of Nigeria (CBN) or the Federal Ministry of Finance – just as the US Department of Treasury owns the office of Terrorism and Finance Intelligence (OTFI). Another Ministry that should have intelligence agency is the Ministry of Defence which should have Defence Intelligence Service (DIS). The American DoD has it own Departmental Intelligence Agency, Defence Intelli-gence Agency (DIA). Meanwhile, the Directorate of Military Intelligence (DMI) should be restructured to the extent that all military services, as already noted, should have separate Intelligence Agencies such as Naval Intelligence Service (NIS) for the Navy and Air Intelligence Agency (AIA) for the Air force. The Army may retain the DMI.

5. Weak State Syndrome

Nigeria is a weak state and that is why it harbours a lot of social actors whose activities compromise its national security. The nature of insecurity dilemma confronting weak states is largely a function of the structural conditions of their existence. They lack the most fundamental of state attributes which concern the existence of effective institutions, a monopoly of the instruments of violence and consensus on the idea of the state (Jackson, 2007). Because they have incomplete or quasi-state, they face numerous challenges to their authorities from powerful domestic actors.

Different measures, though controversial, are actually adopted to assess state strength in order to discover the ones that fall under the category of weak states. Distinguishing between two forms of state power – despotic power and infrastructural power – C. Thomas (1989) links state strength and weakness with institutional capacity. Despotic power concerns the state's coercive abilities and the exercise of force to impose its rule on the people. On the other hand, infrastructural power refers to the effectiveness and legitimacy of the state's institutions and its ability to rule through consensus. In the light of the above, strong states have little need to exercise coercive power because their infrastructural power does not make room for that. Conversely, "the more a weak state exercises coercive power, the more it reinforces its weakness and corresponding lack of infrastructural power" (Jackson, 2007:149). For Barry Buzan (1983:67), weak states "either do not have, or have failed to create, a domestic political and social consensus of sufficient strength to eliminate large scale use of force as a major and continuing element in the domestic political life of the nation". As a counterpoint to the formulations of Thomas and Buzan, J. Migdal (1998) defines state strength in terms of state capacity or the ability of state leaders to use the agencies of the state to get people in the state to do what they want them to do.

The most fundamental feature of weak states is their near inability to establish and maintain a monopoly of the instruments of violence; they share this important mark of nationhood and sovereignty with other domestic actors. These are social actors and they include rival politicians with their own private armies, warlords, criminal gangs, locally organized militias, armed and organized ethnic or religious groups and private security companies and mercenary groups. Therefore, weak states face serious threats from these strongmen. In many cases, these social actors merely organize themselves for self-defence since they cannot be protected by the state which conversely employs excessive coercion.

The choice for Nigeria is clear: it has to identify those elements that conspire to make a country strong and begin to use them for greatness and active peace. In this direction, the first step is to justify and protect its sovereignty. The term *sovereignty* means *omnipotence* – all powerful. "A sovereign has an absolute authority over its jurisdiction and its domestic affairs. Sovereignty cannot be shared with anybody, thus it is indivisible" (Chatterjee, 2007:40). The equivalent of the attributes of absoluteness and indivisibility of the sovereign God on earth is government and therefore government ought not to share its sovereignty with social actors just as God cannot share His with Satan.

Sovereignty is territorial and to this extent, within its boundaries, its jurisdiction-authority remains unchallenge-able (Chatterjee, 2007). Thus, Nigeria should live up to the expectations of governmental *omnipotence* by strengthening itself in all departments of its existence.

6. Democratic Insecurity and Dilemma

Democracy is not the best form of government. Theocracy and monarchy are evidently better than democracy but because they are irrational systems where few individuals play God and constrict ingenuity and creativity, then democracy being a people-based system is always given the pride of place. Democracy is characterized by a lot of oppositional forces and when not played according to rules, it is not only deadly but also anarchical in nature; evidently worse than the worst authoritarianism. Because of features of opposition, its operation is always marked by conflicts and crisis. That is why a society that operates democracy must of necessity embrace key elements of conflict resolution and crisis management because conflict and crises are natural outcomes of political rivalries. These elements include dialogue, negotiation, conciliation, consensus and reconciliation. Besides, key institutions associated with democracy should also be strengthened. These include political parties, civil societies, the court, the press and the security services like the police.

A greater part of the spiral of insecurity in Nigeria is associated with the way the country operates its democracy. The scale of assassinations and ruins associated with nomination exercises and election proper in the country is simply appalling; it is more than the scale of destruction wrought by the activities of insurgents, anarchists and armed robbers put together. Therefore, to achieve peace through democracy, Nigeria should deepen and broaden its democratic space.

CHAPTER TWO

The Boko Haram Phenomenon

Historical Parallels to the Understanding of the Phenomenon of Boko Haram in Northern Nigeria

There are a few historical parallels to the understanding of the phenomenon of Boko Haram in Northern Nigeria and the GON must come to terms with them in order to tackle the challenges effectively. The parallels are a combination of time, season and events in Nigerian History.

1. **Eleventh to Eighteenth Centuries: Episode I**: Islam was introduced into Borno Empire in the eleventh Century and in Hausaland in the fourteenth Century from Mali but it gained hold in the fifteenth Century during the reign of Mohammed Rumfa of Kano (1463 – 99). Between that Century and eighteenth Century it was predominantly the religion of the palace and adherents were oppressed by the court through provocative, oppressive and reprehensible policies. By the eighteenth Century, they (adherents) had started to react to the oppressive tendencies of the court.

2. **Nineteenth Century: Episode I**: In the early years of the nineteenth Century, the scale of oppression in the region had galvanized adherents into action through a Jihad which was led in 1804 by one of the legendary figures in Nigerian history, Usman dan Fodio. The basic aim of the Jihad was to put an end to oppression and syncretism.

The immediate result of the Jihad was the establishment of the Sokoto Caliphate and the spread of Islam in most parts of Northern Nigeria and sub-Saharan Africa. Since the Sokoto Jihad, there was no Jihad in sub-Saharan Africa that did not have the imprimatur of Sokoto (Akpan, 2010).

3. **Nineteenth Century: Episode II**: The British imperialism showed its teeth and bared its fangs in the dying years of this Century and succeeded in creating Nigeria as a state, but in administering this state, Northern Nigeria was largely insulated from Western European and Southern Nigerian influence. This policy was the prelude to social crisis in Nigeria.

4. **Twentieth Century: Episode I**: Whereas in Southern Nigeria, Christian Missionaries had established a number of primary schools which had about 100,000 pupils by 1910; with the Ijebu province alone having 4000, in the entire Northern Nigeria, there were less than 1,000 pupils. These pupils were mostly found in the Christian areas of the North.

With regards to secondary schools, by 1957, the entire north had 41 secondary schools with a total enrolment of 3,643 students, whereas the south had 842 secondary schools with 28,208 students (Sha & Choji, 2011).

5. **Twentieth Century: Episode II**: In the dying days of the colonial administration in Nigeria, attempts were made by the British government to correct the anomalies observable in the social climate of Nigeria through a financial package for the North (See Appendix B). There is no document in any Archive or Museum to show that this package ever came into fruition.

6. **Twentieth Century: Episode III:** Nigeria achieved independence with a suffocating social climate, especially in the North. Political independence presented Nigeria with the golden opportunity to embark on effective nation-building, which is the creation of a state inhabited by an integrated and contented people. This was not to be. Brigandage and imperial politics of the first republic, imperial governance of the Army Generals and imperial democratic credentials of the second, third and fourth republics have combined to send Nigeria into (full) imperial decline where individuals and groups have become social actors, with Boko Haram as just one of the many. In this state of affairs, globalization, weak institutions,

and anarchical state of security, including porous international borders have combined to make the Nigerian case a complete and tragic dilemma.

7. **Miscellaneous Parallels: Episode I**: In Islam, faith and politics and religion and society are intertwined and inseparable. Therefore, even if a country, like Nigeria, is a secular state, a careful balancing act should be struck with adherents of different religions to allow them to practice aspects of their religions based on international best practices, conventional and humanitarian norms and protection of the rights of man. Religion is a cultural issue which cannot ever be separated from man. Security itself partly concerns the absence of existential threats to core values in which religion is a sensitive aspect.

8. **Miscellaneous Parallels**: **Episode II**: The basic principles of Muslim political economy resolve around welfarism, equity, quality, egalitarianism, and charity. These principles are against rentier economies like the one practiced in Nigeria, corruption (most especially financial crimes), lawlessness, oppression, neglect, and child slavery like the *Almajiri* institution in Nigeria. This means that in predominantly Muslim communities, positive peace particulars should be practiced in order to have peace and negative conflict triggers should be outlawed in order not to have conflicts.

The import of the episodes is that the phenomenon of Boko Haram is a horror from the past; a horror that is given contemporary life and strength by the curious and rather outlandish nature of the political economy of Nigeria. It will take strategic engagements and a re-designed political economy to exorcise it from the country; not bullets, name-calling and spurious tag of terrorism.

Boko Haram and the Tag of Terrorism

There is no terrorism in Nigeria and Boko Haram is not a terrorist group but a social actor. Terrorism is a word that does not have

61

acceptable definition. Therefore, as Brenda Lutz and James Lutz (2007:292) argue:

> There has been a multitude of definitions used for terrorism, partially because of disagreements among commentators or analysts and partially because some definers seek to exclude groups that they support or to include groups that they wish to denounce. Courts and police agencies require definitions that permit prosecution and incarcera-tion; political leaders may have different needs and agendas.

However, for John T. Rourke (2008:316), terrorism is

(1) violence;
(2) carried out by individuals, non-governmental organizations, or covert government agents or units; that
(3) specifically targets civilians;
(4) uses clandestine attack methods, such as car bombs and hijacked airliners, and
(5) Attempts to influence politics.

This definition asserts that terrorism focuses on harming some people in order to create fear in others by targeting civilians and facilities or systems (such as transportation) on which civilians rely (Kydd & Walter, 2006).

Brenda Lutz and James Lutz (2007:292) provide a working definition which they argue is relatively neutral in that it recognizes the basic fact that terrorism is a tactic used by different kinds of groups. Their definition includes six major elements. Accordingly, terrorism involves (1) the use of violence or threat of violence (2) by an organized group (3) to achieve political objectives. The violence (4) is directed against a target audience that extends beyond the immediate victims, who are often innocent civilians. Further, (5) while a government can either be the perpetrator of violence or the target, it is only considered an act of terrorism if the other actor is not a government. Finally, (6) terrorism is a weapon of the weak (Lutz & Lutz, 2005:7).

Curiously, this definition excludes kidnappings for financial gain and excludes acts of individuals, even those with political objectives (Lutz & Lutz, 2007). But Eric Neumayer and Thomas Plumper

(2010:313) include kidnapping and a series of acts of violence in their conceptualization of terrorism. According to the duo:

> Acts of terror include, among others, assassina-tions, bombings and armed attacks, arson and fire, kidnapping and skyjacking, unless they are acts of ordinary crime or the violence is for purposes other than political (e.g. for drug trafficking purposes), and unless the violence is committed during international and civil wars. Attacks by guerrilla groups are only included if they inflict damage on civilian targets or dependent of military personnel.

Indeed, the definition of terrorism is largely determined by the definer – and his or its interests. For this reason the US Federal Bureau of Investigation (FBI) defines terrorism as: "The unlawful use of force or violence against persons or property to intimidate or coerce a government, the civilian population, or any segment, thereof, in furtherance of political or social objectives" (Hoffman, 1998:14). Similarly, the US Department of Defence (DOD) defined terrorism in 1990 as: "The unlawful use of, or threatened use, of force or violence against individuals or property to coerce and intimidate governments or societies, often to achieve political, religious, or ideological objectives" (see Falk, 2003:76).

In response to narrow-minded and self-opinionated manners that terrorism is defined, Richard Falk (2003:76) summarizes the position of most scholars on the subject matter of terrorism thus:

> In contrast, any academic specialists, especially critics of US foreign policy over the years, reject such definitional closure, insisting that whenever political violence is directed against those who are "innocent" there exists terrorism, and whoever is the actor is properly charged with terrorism. From this perspective, states are the major terrorist organizations operating on the planet, responsible for the overwhelming majority of civilian deaths from terrorism. The United States itself has extremely dirty hands considering the direct and indirect support that it has given over many years to governments that use oppressive violence against civilian targets. It is worth noting here that dictionary definitions of terrorism avoid confining the term to anti-state violence. For instance, consider the definition provided by the American Heritage College Dictionary: "The unlawful or threatened use of force or violence to intimidate or coerce societies or governments, often for political or ideological reasons".

Political scientists generally tend to restrict terrorism to acts of violence carried out by non-state actors against civilians. Historians, sociologists and international humanitarian lawyers tend to use broader definition that includes all premeditated acts of violence against civilians, whether carried out by non-state political groups or by the state. Indeed, historians go further to look at the cause-effect nature of terrorism. Yet, in general contrast, the non-state entrepreneurs of violence consider their actions to be legitimate forms of resistance to state terrorism aimed at suppressing self-determination, even though civilians may be the immediate targets.

Though no acceptable international convention addresses the issue, the notion of a legitimate right to resist state oppression is controversial. The UN does not help matters in this direction either. Quite often, non-state groups cite the 1960 UN General Assembly Resolution (see UN Papers) on the Granting of Independence to colonial countries and peoples as acknowledging their rights of resistance. Pointedly, the resolution declares that: *forcible resistance to forcible denial of self-determination ... is legitimate. It even goes further to state that non-state actors may receive external support from external sources like governments.*

In the final analysis, terrorism should be seen as a part of the current language game used by statists to describe their adversaries. It is borrowed from the semantic terrain of the American and Israeli Think-Tank militarists and strategists.

Writing about a part of the history of terrorism and highlighting its contemporary twist, Richard Falk (2003:76) documents:

Historically ... the use of terrorism as a term to describe political violence was initially and mainly used to describe governmental violence intended to pacify social forces in a turbulent period, most classically, in the French Revolution. Anti-state violence was more commonly associated with "anarchism". But gradually in the last half-Century statists succeeded in branding their adversaries as "terrorists," most saliently with respect to Israel's struggles in the Middle East, but also in the 1970s and 1980s in Western European countries, in relation to the radical movements of the left that were seeking to shock consumerist societies into a spasm of anti-capitalist politics. During the Cold War, American think-tank militarists had waged their own wars to control the semantic terrain, relying initially on terms like "guerrilla war" and "counter-insurgency warfare" to describe revolutionary nationalism in the Third World. Gradually, the language games changed, and terrorism was effectively appropriated by Western states, especially the United States and Israel, for use in dealing exclusively with the violence of their enemies, even if the targets were of a military or governmental character. Terrorism became equated in political discourse and the media exclusively with any form of anti-state political violence, and especially in relation to political violence used against civilian targets. What makes this issue retain its significance is that governments have succeeded in having their own violence exempted from the stigma of terrorism, and treated with respect by the media and in public discussion. It is generally discussed in the West as "retaliation" or "counter-terrorism", even "self-defence", implying a reactive and defensive violence that often overlooks the inflamed political context. The locus of terrorism can blur considerably depending on the identity of the party responsible for recourse to violence against civil society.

From the foregoing, a terrorist is a violence entrepreneur who is so classified by the state regardless of his political, social and economic goals.

An extension of the analysis so far on terrorism is that there are broadly two types of terrorism, namely; state terrorism and revolutionary terrorism. State terrorism constitutes actions or inactions of a state or its allies or agents that

1. create fear or panic stations
2. result in violence
3. violate fundamental human rights of the citizens and
4. Generate Internally Displaced Persons (IDPs).

On the other hand, revolutionary terrorism involves the use of violence to change completely and once-and-for-all the political, social and economic systems of a state in order to achieve for the citizens absolute liberty regardless of sex, creed, class or ethnicity.

When the activities of Boko Haram are fitted into the schemas of state or revolutionary terrorism or the historical parallels to its emergence and consolidation, it is not a terrorist group. If there is terrorism in Nigeria, certainly it is not of the revolutionary type.

As already stated, there is no terrorism in Nigeria and Boko Haram is not a terrorist group, but a social actor. Social actors are, technically speaking, individuals or groups that violate the laws of a state. They are basically of two types namely; violence entrepreneurs and socio-political and economic saboteurs, with the latter being the most dangerous for a state. This is so because where the former could engage in serial killings of few individuals at a time, the latter's action(s) could lead to deaths and suffering of millions of citizens at a time and these could in turn lead to state collapse or paralysis. It is the latter's actions that produce the former in most countries, including Nigeria.

Overall, Boko Haram is a frankincense monster that was created by the elite of Northern Nigerian extraction against the background of Nigeria's history, geography, politics and political economy. Therefore, it is a horror from the past; a home-grown horror, which should not be classified as terrorism.

A frankincense monster is a monster that is created but cannot be controlled by its creator(s) because of its hybridization and polysepalous propensities and characterizations. But with adequate restructuring of the Nigerian system, the GON can totally control and then completely exorcize from Nigeria in a satisfactory manner, and once and for all, the phenomenon of Boko Haram.

CHAPTER THREE

Tackling the Phenomenon of Boko Haram in Nigeria

Since 1999, Nigeria has been in a state of war but of low intensity civil war. At least three characterizations (of occurrence) of civil war abound. According to the World Bank Policy Research Report (WBPRR) (2003:54), "civil war occurs when an identifiable rebel organization challenges the government militarily and the resulting violence results in more than 1,000 combat-related deaths, with at least five percent on each side". The Report also argues that:

> Civil war occurs if a group of people forms a private military organization that attacks government forces and ordinary civilians on a large scale and with degree of persistence. The typical such organization has between 500 and 5000 members ...

The most recent understanding of the conditions of civil war in a state comes from the Regan's Interventions in Civil Wars (ICW) dataset updated by Regan, Frank and Aydin in 2010. According to the ICW, civil war refers to "armed combat between groups within state boundaries in which there are at least 200 fatalities" (See Aydin, 2010:54).

Whether one uses one or two or a combination of these explanations to look at the Nigerian case, the fact of the matter is that there is already a civil war in Nigeria. The OPC created the sparks, the MASSOB turned them into flames, the Niger Delta insurgents fed the flames and the Boko Haram has raised the bar of these bloody encounters.

The activities of these groups are aspects of low-intensity and localized warfare. Once they are allowed to raise the intensity through retaliatory and counter-retaliatory schemes, the country's history would crack.

Since the birth of the international system, the world has acknowledged the extraordinary exploits of only Seven Generals. Yet, none succeeded in fighting wars on more than one front. Again, since the beginning of the modern world, no country has survived two full-scale civil wars. The prospect of such survival today is even too dimmed to contemplate when combatants do not measure up to the requirements of the Geneva Convention on warfare but are monsters and shadows on ruinous spree. Therefore, Nigeria must move decisively to scorch once and for all cases of challenges to its authority and sovereignty.

Tactics and Strategies of Conquest without Bullets

The phenomenon of Boko Haram in Nigeria should be tackled tactically and strategically. Abstractly, tactics refers to the arrangements and deployments adopted by forces (which in this case is Nigerian leadership) in battle to gain the maximum advantage from their weapons; that is, Nigerian resources (Fourie, 1998). The strand of strategy to be adopted is total strategy which General Andre Beaufre in his book, An *Introduction to Strategy* defines as:

> ...a comprehensive combination of ways of using the various means ... which a government chooses in a conflict so as to create a set of situations which are untenable for its opponents.

Explaining the import of Beaufre's understanding of total strategy, D.F.S. Fourie (1998:19) writes:

> This should tell you that total strategy flows from a set of broad decisions taken by a government about how to engage in a war or in a conflict short of war such as that known as the **Cold War**. It should remind you that a government engaging in war should not be seen as merely adopting a policy of engaging in war – and then leaving it to the armed forces to fight. On the one hand a government is seen as needing to harness all its means through the coordinating mechanism of the Cabinet, so that means other than military means may be employed. Perhaps this may, as with the Cold War, reduce the danger of recourse to armed force.

In general conflict language, total strategy is the capacity of the government to raise the cost and risk of challenges to its authority and sovereignty. This means that the GON should ultimately turn the operating environments of insurgents and anarchists into hostile environments.

In tackling the phenomenon of Boko Haram, the EXCOF should declare a three year state of emergency on the Nigerian national security system and get the NASS to pass necessary laws, chief among which is the treason law to give bite and teeth to the state of emergency. Nigeria is in a state of mini-civil war (Akpan, 2011) and therefore needs a state of emergency to defeat social actors and treasonists. It is pertinent to note here that, actions of governments that are conventionally illegitimate during peace time would be absolutely legitimate during war time or state of emergency. It is only the psychology of warfare or state of emergency that would correct the Nigerian system.

After the declaration of the state of emergency, the GoN should take tactical and strategic steps to turn the heat on anarchists and treasonists – by creating a Nigerian environment hostile to their operations. These would involve tactical and short-term strategy (for one year), medium term strategy (for two years) and long term strategy (five years and beyond).

Contents of the Tactical and Strategic Plans

A. Tactics and Short Term Strategy, 2012

Golden Jubilee +2 Amnesty. The GON should declare Golden Jubilee Amnesty for a new Nigeria. Because two years have passed after the country's Golden Jubilee Anniversary date, the Amnesty programme should be called the Golden Jubilee plus 2. Nigerian prisons should be emptied and inmates freed to go and "sin no more". For those who surrender guns and ammunitions, regardless of their state of origin, the *Niger Delta Analogy and Treatment* should apply. The Niger Delta Analogy and Treatment concerns the Amnesty Programme for the Resource Control Warriors of the Niger Delta region.

Remarks: There is folly in the wisdom of a goat and there is wisdom in the folly of a sheep. The GON should exhibit the folly of a sheep and profit from its innate wisdom and accompanying peace.

Amnesty as a concept has two related meanings: in the first sense, it is an official statement from government that allows people who have been put in prison for crimes against the state to go free. In the second sense, it means a period of time during which people can admit to a crime or give up weapons without being punished.

The government of Nigeria should declare a Golden Jubilee Amnesty and set free people who have committed crimes against the state between January 1960 - the year of Nigeria's Independence - and December 2010 - the last month of the year of its Golden Jubilee. This would take care of the first sense in which Amnesty is expressed. In the second sense, Nigerians should be asked to surrender their weapons which number in millions to the state for Amnesty and the weapons so surrendered should be bought by government at their market value price.

There are several compelling reasons for a Golden Jubilee Amnesty. In the first place, since Nigeria desires transformation, it should break from the past and start afresh in its reform of the judicial system. Secondly, the general Amnesty would send a signal that a new Nigeria is not only possible but also that the law could be used to sustain it. Thirdly, over 99 percent of the crimes committed by Nigerians over the long period, (1960 to 2010), were engineered by bad governance and therefore the victims should be set free and asked to "sin no more" even as government should equally be asked to "sin no more". Fourthly, and on a more fundamental note, Nigerians from the President, who is very visible, to the villagers who are anonymous should be sensitized to know that in a new Nigeria, the prison could be their new homes.

Alternatively, Nigeria should declare a Centenary Amnesty in 1914 for all prisoners. Nigeria as a state actor came into being in 1914 through the amalgamation of Southern and Northern Nigeria into one; even though it achieved political independence in 1960.

The State and Unauthorized Possession of Weapons

After the declaration of the Golden Jubilee +2 Amnesty, it should be a treasonable offence for citizens of Nigeria and foreigners to be in possession of weapons, except those licensed by law to hold them.

Remarks: Any person caught with weapons should not be granted bail and should ultimately be handed down the highest judicial punishment in Nigeria.

Building of Ward Security Stations

The GON should build in all Wards in Nigeria Security Stations worth a minimum of N20 million each. The stations should house all security and para-military forces (outside the military) in Nigeria. These should include Police, Immigration service, Customs, SSS, Nigerian Drug Law Enforcement Agency (NDLEA), National Agency for Food, Drug Administration and Control (NAFDAC) and even the Standard Organization of Nigeria (SON).

Remarks: With less than 10,000 Wards in Nigeria, the GoN needs less than N200 billion to build these stations.

These stations would check-mate considerably cases of crimes in Nigeria. This implies that all forms of crimes would always be nibbed at the bud at the grassroots levels before they gather capacities to spread and become contagious.

Overall, Security Stations at the Ward level would prevent Nigeria from suffering a loss-of-strength-gradient (LSG), which applies to the security reach of states. LSG has to do with effects of distance on the strength, power, and security reach of states internationally and nationally. As documented by Halvard Buhaug (2010:107):

> The capacity of a country (a.k.a. its national strength) is largest at its home base and declines as the nation moves away … In a domestic setting, the ability of a state to exert authority throughout its territory is determined by the government's capability and its LSG.

Therefore, government capability, especially in a broad-acred Nigeria minus LSG equals zero security; that is, government capability – LSG = zero security.

The LSG is derived from Kenneth Boulding's (1962) model of international power projection. Today, even capable states like the US are largely impeded by distance and can no longer influence significantly distant regions outside the American continent.

Nigeria cannot radiate its power and security resources from capitals and headquarters of tiers of governments, which are quite distant from local communities where insecurity dilemma are generated, and hope to be on top of security situations.

To prevent the current situation where the country is a victim of LSG at the national level, all Wards in Nigeria should have fully-equipped security stations.

Ban on Unauthorized Organizations

Within the emergency period, all unregistered social, economic and political organizations should be banned. Therefore, before organizations operate in the country, they should be registered by the Corporate Affairs Commission and these include religious organizations

Remarks: The security operatives should take trend and threat assessments of all non-governmental organizations in Nigeria and determine which ones present threats to national security. The threat assessment should be a yearly affair.

Islamic Banking

Nigeria should establish special banks in all Wards in Nigeria and they should run on the principles of Islamic Banking. They should be called *Ward Banks*. In simple terms, Islamic Banking runs on the basic principles that:

> …interest should not be charged on loans used for the relief of human needs but that this restriction did not apply to loans for business purposes. As the latter were designed to bring profit to the borrower … (Smith, 1958:217).

Until the Italians started lending money with interest in the Middle Ages, both Christianity and Islam in unison rejected usury. As Professor Eno Ikpe (2000:77) has asserted:

> … In the Middle Ages money lending was disapproved of by the Church as usury and no Christian was supposed to take part in it. Thus, the Jews monopolized this branch of business. However, from the fourteenth century, Christians were increasingly taking interest and part in this lucrative business. In the Renaissance period Italian families such as the **Visconti** and the **Medici** began to lend money as a business enterprise. The influence wielded by these families helped to make banking for profit a respectable economic pursuit. In the sixteenth century, banking spread from

Italy into Germany... The development of banking facilitated the rise of various types of aids for large-scale financial transactions – promissory notes, drafts, cheques, etc. The use of cheques greatly facilitated exchange because the credit resources of banks could be expanded far beyond the actual cash available. The growth of trade and industry during the commercial revolution called for more stable and uniform monetary systems. The tendency was for every nation-state of importance to adopt a standard system of money for business within its borders. Commercial and banking business led to the development of new types of professiona-lism.

Usury is as anti-Islam as it is anti-Christianity. If modern capitalism requires some practices of usury on account of profit making where interest, like tax, should be shared, the society should protect those who want to benefit from original religious injunctions.

Remarks: Constituent states should establish *Ward Banks* in all the Wards in their states with a minimum of N10 million each as start up capital. The maximum loan in these Banks for customers should be One Hundred Thousand Naira. In most cases, most people, especially rural women need just Ten Thousand Naira to begin a journey from the poverty line.

Status of Fridays

Fridays in Nigeria should be work free days for government businesses and indeed should be equated with Sundays for Christians and Saturdays for Judaism. Though God's injunctions to Muslims include praying five times daily, Friday is a holy day in Islam and should be appreciated in Nigeria. Commenting further on the status of Fridays for Muslims, Huston Smith (1958:211) writes:

> … While in Islam no day of the week is as sharply set apart from others as is the Sabbath for the Jews or Sunday for the Christians, Friday most nearly approximates a holy day. Formality is not a pronounced feature in Islam but the closest that Muslims come to a formal service of worship is when they gather on Fridays for noon prayers and collective recital of the Koran. These gatherings are usually in mosques, and visitors to Muslim lands testify that one of the most impressive sights in the religions of man occurs when, in a dimly lighted mosque, hundreds of men stand shoulder to shoulder, then kneel and prostrate themselves toward Mecca. The exact answer to where the Muslim should pray however is anywhere …

Remarks: The GON should declare Friday's work-free days. To make up for lost hours, government businesses between Mondays and Thursdays should end at 6.00pm. This would take care of the 8 hours (8.00am – 4.00pm) that would be lost on Fridays.

The school system should end all activities by 10.00am on Fridays but between Mondays and Thursdays, primary and secondary schools should end all academic activities by 3.00pm.

If facilities for tourism are developed in Nigeria, the three free days (that is, Friday, Saturday and Sunday) would promote tourism and the travel industry in general. For the Euro-American World, weekend means Saturday and Sunday; for Nigeria it should denote Friday, Saturday and Sunday.

The tiers of government in Nigeria should turn the Nigerian weekends into weekly *peace and friendship* days. Indeed, if these special days are well managed in Nigeria, they would generate revenues for government to make up for the lost hours of Fridays

Additionally, Nigerian workers rarely go on vacation to renew themselves for enhanced productivity. The proposed Nigerian weekend should be seen as vacation period as well for the workers.

Creation of the Ministries of Charity Affairs

Ministries of Charity Affairs should be created in all the states in the North-East, North-Central and North-West geo-political zones of Nigeria to collect *zakat*. Proceeds from *zakat* should be used for social development of the people of the regions. There may be the need to establish Social Development Commission in each of these states and the focus of the Commission should be on the development of the educational and health institutions in these two regions. The development of special and entrepreneurial skills of the youths of the region should also be the focus of the Commission.

Remarks: States in the North East and North-West geo-political zones, especially, should emulate the Saudi Arabian example where *zakat* is an instrument of wealth creation and income distribution as well as revenue for government and the funding of charitable works.

On these matters, the Report of the 9/11 Commission in the US, also called the Kean Commission (2008:423) noted:

> Charitable giving, or zakat, is one of the five pillars of Islam. It is broader and more pervasive than Western ideas of charity – functioning also as a form of income tax, educational assistance … Funding charitable works is an integral function of the governments in the Islamic world. It is so ingrained in Islamic culture that in Saudi Arabia, for example, a department within the Saudi Ministry of Finance and National Economy collects **zakat** directly, much as the US Internal Revenue Service collects payroll with-holding tax.

If the states of Northern Nigeria had emulated the Saudi example on *zakat* and had used the proceeds for educational development (only, for instance) since independence, the ***Almajiri*** phenomenon would not have existed in Nigeria and certainly the Boko Haram syndrome in the northern half of Nigeria would not have been experienced as well. Therefore, these states should start to do the needful in order to earn for themselves and Nigeria respect, honour, peace, security and development. A good starting point is the creation of the Ministries of Charity Affairs as Institutions of their governments.

General Ban on Motorcycles in State Capitals and Cities

As motorcycles are often used as perfect launching pads to throw bombs around and to shoot on account of their advantages of snaking through traffic, especially in cities, they should be banned.

Remarks: States that have not banned the use of motorcycles in their cities should do so. They may profit from the Akwa Ibom State experience where the state bought motorcycles from owners at a flat rate of Seventy Thousand Naira.

Establishment of Special Forces

The GON, through the NASS, should establish Special Forces from the Air force, Army, Navy and the Police. These should be Air Marshal (from the Air Force), Border Guard (from the Army), Coast Guard (from the Navy) and National Guard (from the Police). Section

214 of the 1999 Constitution gives NASS power to establish these security forces.

Remarks: The first set of the special security forces should be sent on training in Israel, US, Britain, France and South Korea. These are countries that have such Guards.

Specialized Vehicle Plate Numbers

The GON should declare the existing plate numbers of vehicles and motorcycles in Nigeria as expired and take steps to issue specialized security plate numbers within the year.

The plate numbers with security codes should be tied to the owners of vehicles and motorcycles in which case the particulars of the owners should be captured into national data bank. These should include passport, addresses, fingerprints, height, complexion, colour of eye and colour of the vehicles. Under no circumstances should a vehicle or motorcycle use the Nigerian roads without appropriate plate numbers and under no circumstances should owners of vehicles or motorcycles change the colours of these facilities without police permission and without changing the data to reflect the new colours.

There are many external hard drives to contain all these information and a drive like tetra byte can contain all information in the whole wide world. And the good news is that these drives are the size of a human palm and each costs about one hundred dollars. This implies that every security operative can own, and by law operate, one.

Remarks: The GON should give out new plate numbers free of charge but on a condition that owners of vehicles or motorcycles to benefit from the scheme should possess valid documentation with regards to road worthiness, up-to-date tax particulars, insurance cover for the vehicles and motorcycles, valid licences and other documents on road taxes.

The GON would be amazed to know that if it spends billions of Naira to provide these plate numbers, the three tiers of government would earn trillions of Naira through proper documentation of these facilities.

After the exercise, any operator of vehicles or motorcycles without specialized plate number and up-to-date valid documents should be charged for treason. Like in the case of the US, registration of vehicles in Nigeria should be annual exercise. The US model is a defence model which would strengthen security of Nigeria.

New National Identity Card Scheme

The GON should embark on a new ID card scheme and under no circumstances should a Nigerian of 12 years old and above live in Nigeria without ID card particulars, which should be fed into the national data bank.

Like in the case of vehicle numbers, the scheme should capture sensitive particulars like height, complexion, colour of the eye, age, addresses, fingerprints etc.

These information could equally be contained in hard drives like tetra bytes which could be possessed by security operations.

False Information and Documentation should attract treasonable charges and punishment as well. Once deviants like anarchists and insurgents move with vehicles and motorcycles with specialized plate numbers, they would be highly vulnerable.

Remarks: Even if the scheme costs the nation N1 trillion, the GON should embark on it speedily. Deviants, all over the world, are scared of database that contains everything about them. It cannot be anything else in Nigeria.

Under no circumstances should a Nigerian of 13 years and above live in Nigeria without having a proper national identity card.

Re-Registration of SIM Cards

Once deviants communicate, they are vulnerable (Akpan, 2005). Therefore, one wonders why the country is seriously menaced by anarchists and insurgents in the era of the General System for Mobile (GSM) communications in Nigeria. It means that Nigeria does not use the GSM facilities to provide itself with security. Even when the country embarked on the registration of SIM cards in 2011, it never did the exercise with security consciousness in mind. It was done in the most lackadaisical manner and up till today SIM cards are sold on the streets without security inputs and by persons without security permission.

Therefore, the GON through the office of the National Security Adviser (NSA) should re-register all SIM cards and create a national security database for security purposes in the country.

Remarks: Under no circumstances should any citizen operate the GSM with SIM cards that are not registered and captured in the national database.

It should amount to treasonable offence for anybody to operate GSM in the country in which the SIM is not registered.

Licensing and Operations of Local Radio Stations

Communication is the foremost instrument of conflict resolution and crisis management. Therefore, the GON should give Radio Licences to its 774 LGCs to operate community radio stations with local contents of more than 50 percent.

Remarks: The Radio Stations should be regulated by the National Broadcasting Corporation (NBC) but should be built by the various LGCs.

Declaration of Crude Oil and Associated Gas as National Commons

The GON should declare the country's Crude oil and associated gas as national commons and or common heritage to be shared equally by the constituent states. This implies that the 13 percent derivation for the oil producing states should be thrown into the dustbin of history. Of course, Crude oil and Associated gas should be declared as *national commons* based on the following conditions:

1. 10 percent of Crude oil and Associated gas proceeds, in dollars, should be given to the LGCs where these resources are produced. Host communities should be defined as the LGCs where oil and gas are mined. By law, the ten percent revenue

should be used for capital projects only in the host communities. These LGCs should, through such funds, be turned into little Monacos.

Monaco is an official sovereign state on the Cote d' Azur (French Reveira) with an area of 1.98 square kilometres, a population of 35,986 and a GDP of $215,163 – the world's highest GDP nominal per capita.

All oil producing LGCs in Nigeria should stand out as little Monacos, but within sovereign and independent Nigeria. By the way, Nigeria can contain 467,000 Monacos.

2. Whereas proceeds from Crude oil *alone* should be shared among the tiers of government and strategic institutions, proceeds from *Associated gas* should be saved at all times as the SWF after 10 percent in dollars is remitted to LGCs where gas is mined.

3. Whereas Crude oil and Associated gas should be declared as *national commons*, solid minerals, liquified gas and condensate should be owned exclusively by the states where the resources are located, not by GON anymore, and 10 percent of proceeds of production should similarly be given to the LGCs where the minerals are located.

If the states are allowed to own, regulate and exploit solid minerals, liquefied gas and condensate, while the GON collects tax on these sources, in addition to crude oil and Associated gas that it would solely regulate, the states and by implication Nigeria would be paradise for investors and an average annual investment per state would be in excess of $5 billion, which is in the region of N1 trillion. For a glance at the arrays of natural resources per state, see Appendix C.

4. The LGCs that host mineral sites should constitutionally be empowered to set environmental and green accounting standards for mining operations within their areas.

79

5. The percentage of derivation should be increased to a minimum of 50 percent in order to make the Nigerian economic environment competitive.

6. The 68 provisions in the Exclusive Legislative List in the 1999 Constitution should be reduced considerably and given to the constituent states and the LGCs.

7. The three arms of the GON should be decentralized; each should be located in Central, Northern and Southern Nigeria. Indeed, Calabar, the first capital of Nigeria, should be made to host the Headquarters of the NASS.

8. Corporate Headquarters of oil firms operating in Nigeria should be re-located to the Niger Delta; Exxon-Mobil to Akwa Ibom State, Shell to Rivers State, Agip to Bayelsa State, Chevron to Delta State, etc.

9. VAT should be collected by individual States and shared with their LGCs; the GON should not partake in it any longer.

10. All states should be entitled to $1 billion from the foreign reserves for special developmental projects.

11. Proceeds from crude oil should statutorily be used for capital budgets of all the tiers of governments in Nigeria; recurrent expenditures of the tiers of governments should be based on non-oil proceeds and taxes.

12. Calabar and Lagos Island should be entitled to N1 trillion each from the GON as compensation for hosting Nigerian Capital in both colonial and post-independence Nigeria.

13. A minimum of N1trillion should be set aside by the GON for search for oil and gas in the northern region of Nigeria.

14. Extra revenue from the declaration of crude oil and associated gas as national commons should be used by non-oil producing states in only three key areas of economic development, namely: Agriculture, Tourism and Solid Minerals.

It is worth noting that Nigeria has four oil basins with only one, the Niger Delta basin, being given serious attention at the moment. Three other basins are the Lake Chad basin which stretches from the Republic of Chad into Borno, Yobe and Bauchi States in Nigeria; the Benue Trough which covers the states of Benue, Nasarawa, Kogi and

Niger; and the Rima basin, which stretches from Niger Republic into Nigerian states of Katsina, Kebbi, Sokoto and Zamfara.

The Republics of Chad and Niger which share these basins with Nigeria have since discovered oil and gas in commercial quantities in the own sides of the basins; Nigeria ought not to go empty-handed in its own sides of the basins.

With a grant of N1 trillion to search for oil in Northern Nigeria, the prospects of oil find in this region would become brighter and the Nigerian economy would be better for it.

Remarks: The declaration would require constitutional amendments to accommodate conditions under which Crude oil and Associated gas become national commons. The Amendment of the relevant Sections of the Constitution should be carried out immediately.

There is nothing in logic, historical experience (as the cases of the Niger and Chad Republics show) or even geological properties of some states in Northern Nigeria to assume that oil and gas cannot be found in Northern Nigeria. Niger and Chad (which have oil and gas) border Northern Nigeria and share same geological characteristics.

What could be the implication of the new regime for the Niger Delta States, the only region that provides economic life-line for Nigeria? Once these states control their Condensate, Liquified gas, Solid Minerals and VAT solely and get additional resources from the other twenty seven states, which would now have some resources to bring to the centre for sharing, unlike the present situation that they bring zero figure, those in the big league like Akwa Ibom, Rivers, Delta and Bayelsa will have a minimum of N1 trillion for their budgets, while the rest will have a minimum of N500 billion. In the case of Rivers State, for example, the annual value of its LNG at Bonny is $5 billion; about N800 billion. The same applies to Bayelsa State with its LNG. Akwa Ibom State can earn much from its condensate. For Lagos state, VAT alone means a minimum of N1 trillion for its annual budget.

The reality analysis of the new regime for the non-oil states is that they will have a minimum of N500 billion for their annual budgets. Therefore, a declaration of crude oil and associated gas as national commons would mean the unlocking of boundless economic opportunities for the states of Nigeria; in addition to oil-producing communities which would go the *Monaco* way. All of these are the embodiments of functional resource control; resource control with a human face.

Retooling of SURE

The focus and style of SURE should be retooled. The money from SURE should be used to develop five related projects, namely (1) Pipelines of fuel and gas to every state capital and water from the South to the North (2) Water transportation (3) Dams (4) Greenery projects in the environment sector across Nigeria (5) Railway lines across the States of Nigeria.

Remarks: The present focus and style of SURE are like that of the Jack of all trade and master of none. It is a black hole approach to development.

Commencement of the Making of a New Constitution

The 1999 Constitution of Nigeria reinforces imperial politics, imperial administration and imperial democracy. It should not surprise any citizen that imperial politics and administration have caused imperial overstretch and have quickened the processes of imperial decline under which mutation of social actors like Boko Haram have taken place. Therefore, the country desires, and quickly too, a democratic Constitution and not strings of military decrees which the 1999 Constitution is.

The 1999 Constitution may be amended year in, year out but it would not give the nation superlative results. For Nigeria to overcome imperial decline, the *Nigerian Reform Commission* should be convocated by the President to give Nigeria a new Constitution.

On a more fundamental note, there must be a way of getting Nigerians to be productive and oil should be the foundation of production in the country. Unfortunately, oil will never fulfil that role for the country except Nigeria embarks on fundamental political and economic restructuring of the country and agrees on *common fundamentals*. Right now, it is a twisted state and, in fact, a mere legal fiction; a country without citizens, laws and governments.

There are two ways of embarking on the restructuring of the country and these are dialogue and negotiation. But these cannot be done in a vacuum. Therefore, there is need for a political platform for dialogue and negotiation. A lot of people are of the view that the country should embark on the convocation of a Sovereign National Conference as a platform for dialogue in order to reach the desired agreements on *common fundamentals*. The Sovereign National Conference approach is a recipe for confusion and anarchy because there would be no acceptable formula on how to get the representatives for the Conference. Since Nigeria has National Assembly (NASS) in place where every Nigerian is represented, the NASS should turn itself into *Nigeria Reform Commission* and the Nigeria Governors' Forum (NGF) and Chairmen of the Association of Local Government of Nigeria (ALGON) in each of state of the federation should be co-opted into the Commission. This would be a kind of Supper Commission (Suppercom).

The Senate President and the Chairman of the Governors' Forum should be joint Chairmen of the Commission and the Speaker of the House of Representatives and the National President of ALGON should be joint Vice Chairmen.

The Commission should give Nigeria a future with a strategic roadmap away from vulnerable systems that abound everywhere in the country. Politically, there is dire need for devolution of power and the need to streamline relations between the three tiers of government with the LGCs being completely independent and autonomous. The FDDs, SFDs and SDDs strategic pathways should be incorporated into the relations. There is also need to structure the country's federalism to suit the country's aspirations with regards given to its multi-ethnic and multi-religious backgrounds.

Remarks: The convocation of the Nigerian Reform Commission should take place as soon as possible.

General Remarks

If the tactical and short-term strategic requirements are embarked upon, the murderous activities of Boko Haram would recede and its phenomenon would be at bay.

83

A six month period is enough to achieve the tactical and short-term strategic requirements. Nigeria is bleeding and, therefore, the GON has to mobilize the citizenry to rise to the occasion.

The tactical and short-term strategic requirements should be accompanied by sustained propaganda and the ***accidents of populism and bravado technique*** should be employed immediately. This concerns tragedic-melodrama associated with populism.

Two examples are typical. In the al Qaeda experience, Osama bin Laden mobilized Muslims to fight against the United States and the West and he; "consistently characterized his targets as 'crusaders', referring to the Christian occupiers of the Holy Land between the eleventh and thirteen centuries" (Sorenson, 2008:3). When George W Bush, the President of America first code-named his campaign against al Qaeda as a "crusade" after the September 11 attacks, majority of youths in the Muslim World justified the al Qaeda campaign. Though the US quickly retracted the statement, the damage had already been done. But when the deaths were counted and it was realized that for every Euro-American killed, hundreds of Arabs were killed and the scale of destruction of the Arab World, especially Iraq was unquantifiable in relations to the al Qaeda capacity to inflict damages on America, the al Qaeda phenomenon receded. Even some Muslim states started to hunt al Qaeda in their states. Therefore, the tragedy associated with the al Qaeda phenomenon in the Arab World somewhat tamed the monster to the extent that it did not have the capacity to hijack the Arab spring.

The other experience of the accidents of populism and bravado took place in Nigeria. That was the first coup d'état. The coup was welcomed everywhere especially in the northern part of Nigeria, but when the deaths were counted and the territory in which the coup was hatched was considered, it was found out that groups from particular regions wrecked havoc on groups in other regions. This realization ended the celebration of the coup in the North and from that moment the coup plotters were hunted.

Therefore, Nigerians in Northern Nigeria should realize that they are the immediate targets and victims of the orgiastic taste and excesses of Boko Haram and not the South and Southerners. This calls for the mobilization of Nigerians to rout the phenomenon. The GoN has a major role to play by empowering the people of the region to become *security humans*, especially in the sensitive and critical area of intelligence. This re-enforces the need for all LGCs in Nigeria to have radio stations and the US experience strengthens this need.

In the aftermath of 9/11 in the US, the Kean Commission that probed the 9/11 Intelligence Failure recommended that the US must do more to communicate its message. And reflecting on Bin Laden's success in reaching Muslim audiences, Richard Holbrooke wondered: "How can a man in a cave out-communicate the world's leading communication society?" Deputy Secretary of State Richard Armitage added that he was worried that Americans had been; "exporting our fears and our anger", not our vision of opportunity and hope (Kean Commission, 2007:425). Nigeria should, therefore, consolidate its vision of opportunity and hope to Nigerians through credible media platforms, including Radio Stations in all the LGCs and not through JTFs. Its media Executives should out-communicate the Boko Haram Executives.

B. Medium Term Strategy, 2013 – 2014
Presidential Doctrine of 50:50

The Budgets of 2013 across the three tiers of government should reflect a Presidential Doctrine of 50 percent for Recurrent Expenditure and 50 percent for Capital Expenditure.

A credible option to this doctrine is that all tiers of government in Nigeria should by law be made to use revenues from oil exclusively for capital budgets while non-oil proceeds and taxes should be used for recurrent expenditures.

A useful adjunct to this doctrine is that all tiers of government and their establishments, institutions and agencies should purchase and use only vehicles assembled in Nigeria in order to create jobs, stimulate the vehicle industry and encourage the patronage of made-in-Nigeria goods.

Remarks: The Presidential Doctrine will change the direction of development in Nigeria from rentier pole towards the active peace pole and this would make mobilization of Nigerians for higher goals possible.

Establishment of FDDs, SDDs and SFDs

The GON in league with other tiers of government in Nigeria should establish Federal Development Districts (FDDs), State Development Districts (SDDs), and Special Federal Districts (SFDs). As soon as practicable, all federal constituencies should be turned into FDDs; all Wards in Nigeria into SDDs and all frontier LGCs into SFDs.

Remarks: The creation of FDDs, SDDs and SFDs would promote security in Nigeria, mobilization of the citizens for development, creation of jobs and wealth and reduction in economic sabotage.

No human being should live in, enter or pass through any SFD without possessing a valid National Identity Card and if the person is a foreigner, a valid international passport.

Establishment of Nigerian Overseas Development Fund

Nigeria should use 10 percent of the proceeds from its oil to establish Nigerian Overseas Development Fund (NODEF) to assist African countries in Africa and in the Diaspora.

The first beneficiaries should be the contiguous states where the SFDs should be replicated in these countries with money from the Fund.

Remarks: With NODEF Nigeria would extend its security blanket from its SFDs into the outer frontiers of the neighbouring states.

The blanket would cover Nigeria and the contiguous states as well. SDFs would check flows of SALWs into Nigeria and the movement of fleeing rebels like Boko Haram to and from the contiguous states.

Decentralization of the Police

As soon as practicable, Nigeria should start the process of the decentralization of the Police. This should result in the creation of State Police, Local Government Police and Establishment Police for higher institutions and Banks.

The contemporary security challenges in Nigeria require urgent decentralization of the Nigeria police and that specifically means that

86

all three tiers of government should have their police establishments. In addition, all higher educational institutions in the country should have their police establishments. The same should apply with regards to international, national and regional banks that have branches in all states in the country plus the Central Bank of Nigeria (CBN).

Meanwhile, the GON should retain the Police Mobile Force, whose designation should be changed to National Guard (NG), the states should be made to retain the regular police and the Local Government system should have the Road Marshals and Local Government Police which should be called *Neighbourhood Police* (NP). In Itu LGC in Akwa Ibom, for instance, the police establishment should go by the name Itu Neighbourhood Police and in Biu LGC in Borno state. The police outfit should be known as Biu Neighbourhood Police. Altogether, security agencies operated by the LGCs should not exceed 1000 per LGC.

Nigeria should retool its security and police systems in the light of new challenges. It may have to take a cue from the United States of America. In the aftermath of the 9/11 attack on the US, the country came to the simple conclusion that it needed a different way of organizing the government. Specifically, the Kean Commission (2007:437) reported that: "Those attacks showed, emphatically, that ways of doing business rooted in a different era are not just good enough. Americans should not settle for incremental, ac hoc adjustments to a system designed generations ago for a world that no longer exists".

Drawing lessons from the American response to the 9/11 episode, it should be noted that the phenomenon of Boko Haram in Nigeria is a typical generational challenge that requires a multiple layered security system as no single security measure is fool proof. In terms of policing, the existence of only the Federal police system is nothing other than continuous romance with collective vulnerability. The argument that other tiers of government do not deserve police establishments is simply a Neanderthal argument. Nigeria has three tiers of governments to start with and all are in the business of making laws for the good of the citizens. Yet a critical test of laws lies in enforceability; otherwise they are not worthier than the papers on which they are printed. The Federal police system alone is largely inadequate for Nigeria. In any case Nigeria does not deserve such a structure; the country is operating now in a world that no longer exists. A new world in which citizens are their country's immediate enemies require grassroots approach to policing and a soaking technique to respond to deviants. Deviants hardly operate in environments that are soaked with security operatives. A new security world for Nigeria requires the decentralization of the police system.

Remarks: The decentralization of the Police system will bring about perfect security in Nigeria as deviants cannot knock off heterogeneous police system unlike the current (Nigerian) homogenous system that guarantees collective vulnerability.

The word **Police** should never be heard of again in democratic Nigeria at the national level from 2020, but in the states and LGCs. The Police Mobile Force should be replaced by the National Guard, which along with other paramilitary and intelligence services should enforce federal laws. State Police should enforce state laws in the states while the Neighbourhood Police; that is, LGC Police system should enforce LGC laws.

With clearly delineated boundaries, deviants who violate the laws of any tiers of government should be arrested by any police establishment but they should be handed over to law enforcement agents in charge of enforcement of specific laws. Thus, the National Guard could arrest anybody who violates the laws of the LGC in which he operates from, but hands him over to the Neighbourhood Police of the LGC. In a similar vein, the State Police could arrest a violator of the law of a particular LGC in the state, but hands him over to Neighbourhood Police of that particular LGC for prosecution. This way, the robustness of the police system would be preserved and consolidated.

To be sure, there is fear of abuse of state police by Governors given their imperial tendencies but with enough constitutional safeguards and checks and balances, the fear would be highly misplaced. In the first place, Nigeria should establish an Independent Police Complaints' Commission (IPCC) to treat cases of police high-handedness for redress and justice (Akpan, 2011).

One critical condition for State police should be the removal of full immunities for State Governors. Nigeria is about the only country in the wide world where domestic actors are entitled to immunities.

Immunities are of diplomatic origin and are meant for international or intermestic actors, which Nigerian Governors are certainly not. Only four intermestic actors in Nigeria should be entitled to immunities, namely; the President, the Vice President, the First Lady and the Minister of Foreign Affairs; the last two outside Nigeria only. They alone are also entitled to the use of His/Her Excellency – as the title too is meant for international or intermestic actors – while Governors are entitled to the designation of His/Her Honour. Thirdly, in addition to the IPCC, there should be the establishment of the Human Rights Court of Justice in Nigeria to take care of human rights violation that may arise from the police and, indeed, all security forces and governmental agencies in the country. Fourthly, the maximum number of police personnel that a state should have at any point in time should not exceed 10,000. Fifthly, the State, Neighbourhood and establishment police organizations should be armed with only small arms (and never with light weapons).

A ten year transition period should be initiated where states should start with 1,000 personnel and add 1000 every year until they reach the benchmark. Simultaneously, the Neighbourhood Police establishments should start with 100 personnel and add 100 every year until they reach the needed number of personnel.

The foundation of State and Neighbourhood police establishments should be built on police personnel already in the national police who are from particular states and LGCs and who are not above 50 years of age but have served for a minimum of ten years.

As parts of efforts to contain potential recklessness on the part of State police against non-indigenes, each state should have state representatives in all the states of the federation. Their duties should be the ***domestic equivalents*** of ambas-sadorial duties in foreign countries.

The other fear of state police concerns their manipulation for secession purposes and it is perhaps based on the scale of insurgencies in the country and the demands of the insurgents for separation. But it should be quickly noted that secessionist demands are championed by a negligible fraction of Nigerians even in the insurgents' enclave. There is also the fear based on external observations like the case of the US Institute that Nigeria would break up before too long.

On the contrary, the reality is that: "there is no state or ethnic group in Nigeria that has the capacity to embark on secession successfully. The most any can do is to engineer and embark on large-scale violence, colom-bianization and somalianization of sections of the Nigerian society but not outright secession. In fact, secession cannot succeed in Nigeria because of its ethnic mix and configuration which are rooted in absence of dominance and polarization" (Akpan, 2011:253).

Besides, small arms which these new police establishments are meant to bear are not suitable at all for warfare; modern wars require light and heavy weapons, among others. Additionally, only states that are willing and ready should establish police bodies. Even in the First Republic, only the Northern and Western regions established regional police bodies; in the Eastern region there were no police other than the Nigeria Police Force; that is, the Federal Police.

In any case, with the building of *Security Stations* in all the Wards in Nigeria and the conversion of frontier LGAs into SFDs, all of which would have a mixture of military and para-military forces and security operatives from all the states of the Federation, there is absolutely nothing to fear. To start with, no group can start secession bid if it does not secure external support and guarantee of supply of weapons and spare parts. With SFDs as security rings around Nigeria, no group would be guaranteed these and therefore no group can start the spark of secession.

For funding and operations of the proposed new police structure in Nigeria, see Appendix D

Establishment of Early Warning System in Nigeria

Nigeria should, as a matter of urgency, establish Early Warning System (EWS), which should be designed to detect and respond to early threats and conflict signs. All conflicts, it should be noted, have a gestation period. The challenge of EWS; "is not so much in identifying societies at risk, in general, but in recognizing patterns of change that will lead to the acceleration of conflict" (Nicolaidis, 1996:34).

90

Remarks: EWS should be installed in all Wards in Nigeria. This reinforces the need for security stations in Wards in the country.

There is also the need to create and equip EWS institutions in Nigeria – the Early Warning System Commissions – in the offices of the Local Government Chairman, Governors and the NSA.

Use of Dual-Use Technology to Fight Crime

Nigeria should procure and deploy dual-use technology, especially in urban centres, to fight crime. Dual-use technology is technology that has peaceful uses in addition to military applications.

Remarks: There are a number of dual-use technologies that can detect bombs, explosive guns and weapons generally from a distance between few metres and a kilometre.

Such weapons should be used by security operatives to raise the cost and risk of committing crimes in Nigeria, especially heinous ones.

Withdrawal of the Military from the Streets of Nigeria

The military power may be one critical instrument that provides the sword for policy-makers and the military itself may be an instrument of conflict resolution and foreign policies of nations, but in domestic crises other than full scale wars, circumspection should be the rule of the game in the deployment of soldiers. The continued deployment of troops to the streets and choke-points in Nigeria responds to the madman theory. The policy of applying maximum force to levels that have previously been regarded as disproportionate to the conflict and to the objectives of the parties is called the madman theory. The theory has its origins in the Vietnam War. In that war, superiority of weapons disappointed ultimately in war situations. Indeed, in terms of weapons, technology, manpower and financial prowess, the ratio was one is to one-thousand (1:1000) between Vietnam, then a bicycle economy and the US, a superpower, but the US lost the war, an ugly outcome that forces a scholar like Halvard Buhaug (2010:12) to persuasively argue that: "military superiority does not always secure peace and its victorious outcomes of war".

For Nigeria, it should be noted that youths that engage the military in various choke points across the country are not combatants in the sense of the Geneva Convention, but adventurers on bravado showmanship that ordinarily should be contained by the police and forces of economic development. Beyond this, it is worthy of note that; "conventional security doctrines are weak when the enemy is shadowy, shapeless and determined and the objectives are nebulous" (Akpan 2011:160). In a sentence, Nigeria should start a grand process and or scheme of withdrawing soldiers from the streets of Nigeria.

Remarks: Writing on the Chapter entitled The Military Approach and the Search for Peace in the Niger Delta in the book; *The Niger Delta Question and the Peace Plan,* Otoabasi Akpan (2011:161) had documented:

> In asking the military to intervene in the Niger Delta crisis, the country should be mindful of the intimate connection between force and diplomacy. In this direction, it should first profit from the counsel of the great Chinese strategist, Sun Tzu, who wrote about 500 BC that: "A government should not mobilize its army out of anger ... Act when it is beneficial; desist when it is not" (Rourke, 2008:326). Secondly, it should note that wars should be governed by political, not military, considerations. As Karl Von Clausewitz (1832:8), the father of war, argued:
>
>> War ... is an act of violence which aims at compelling our opponent to do our will ... the goals of military violence, as well as the amount of efforts to be made, will be determined by the political objective, the original motive for the war ... war is not a pastime; not a mere passion for venturing and winning; not the work of free enthusiasm; it is a serious business for a serious object. The war of a community, of entire nations and particularly civilized nations, is always called forth by a political motive in a political situation. It is, therefore, a political act, (and) ... naturally this original motive ... should continue to be the most important consideration in conducting it. Still, the political objective is not a despotic law-giver by that fact alone; it must accommodate itself to the nature of means ... changes in those means may involve a modification in the political objectives, though the latter always must be given first consideration. Policy is intertwined in the whole course of war, and must continually influence it as far as the nature of the forces let loose by war will permit ... a method

which must always include objectives as a part of itself ... war is only a continuation of state policy by other means.

Thirdly, it should be told that war should be fought with clear political goals otherwise disaster looms. As Liddel Hart admonishes nations:

> The object of war is to attain a better peace ... hence, it is essential to conduct war with the constant regard as to the kind of peace we desire, for if we concentrate exclusively on victory, with no thought for the after-effect, we may be too exhausted to profit by peace, while it is almost certain that such peace will be a bad one, containing the germs of another war (Momah, 1995:7).
> Fourthly, it should equally profit from the counsel of Colin Powell, former Chairman of Joint Service Chief of the US that: "Army fight people; police protect people" (Al Jazeera News, February 22, 2010).

The same advice can be generalized on a Nigerian-wide scale without being accused of stage-diving. Again, the **Niger Delta Analogy and Treatment**, based on a once-and-for-all Restoration Agenda, should apply in the attempt to disarm all youths of Nigeria who are on ruinous spree. Even if it costs the nation gargantuan fortune and indeed trillions of Naira to restore these youths, the country should profit from the prophetic imagination of Sun Tzu who opined that the costliest peace is cheaper than the cheapest war.

The Imperative of Making History Subject Compulsory in Secondary Schools

The sum total of the experiences that a nation has can serve as a tonic to spur her up to achieve greatness and by implication confer the status of a leader on that nation in the international system. As a subject, history, which is the study of man and his activities in time perspectives, is very unique among all academic subjects. Its uniqueness lies in the fact that it teaches men about particular events, time and set of men in the past and in an attempt to re-live their lives and conditions, certain pitfalls and dreaded mines are avoided while wonderful achievements of particular eras could be nurtured and consolidated.

With regards to its purposes and utility, they are great and diverse and there is yet no great nation that ignores the lessons of history. According to G. R. Elton, history:

> Enlarges the area of individual experience by teaching about human behaviour, about men in relation to other men, about the interaction of circumstances and conditions and their effects upon individual and social fortunes (see Marwick, 1976:87).

The summation of Trevor-Roper is particularly apt on the value of historical experience to a nation's power. According to him:

> It (historical experience) widens our perspectives by opening our minds to the achievements of other ages and other people and thus helps us to appreciate the limitations of our own view of the world. It forces us, in short, to avoid parochialism (see Marwick 1976:91).

History is an instrument of conflict resolution and crisis management. For one, through history of Nigeria, Nigerians would come to know that a few hundred years ago, they did not live and own the communities they are living and owning today. That centuries before the twentieth were characterized by constant movement of people to new settlements and regions and, therefore, no Nigerian could be classified, strictly speaking, as an indigene or as a settler; all are generational settlers.

Through history Nigerians would come to appreciate a number of limitations in their system. For example, they will come to know that Singapore which boasts of annual budgets in excess of $100 billion does not possess oil and gas and is not as big as any Local Government Area in Nigeria; if Singapore is placed in Nigeria, there would be 1,920 of them as against 774 LGAs in the country. Others in the league of Singapore are Hong Kong, which is the exact size of Ogoniland, and the state of Israel. If Hong Kong and Israel are placed in Nigeria, there would be 884 Hong Kongs and 46 states of Israel. Each boasts of annual budget in excess of $100 billion as against Nigeria's $30 billion for more than 100 million citizens. The population of Singapore is 3 million; that of Hong Kong is 6 million and that of Israel is 8 million. All the 774 LGAs in Nigeria have mineral deposits and are not developed, whereas Singapore and Hong Kong do not have any known mineral but are industrially developed.

The historical transformation of these countries could spur up Nigeria to rise above average possibilities. Presently, Nigerians are lost because they do not know their past, their present and therefore cannot clone the future to work for them.

Ultimately, Nigeria may wish to note the warning of Emeritus Professor of History, Professor Jacob Festus Ade-Ajayi, the doyen of African historiography, who observes that:

> The nation (or state) suffers which has no sense of history; its values remains superficial and ephemeral unless imbued with a deep sense of continuity and a perception of success and achievement that transcends the acquisition of temporary power and transient wealth; such a nation (or state) cannot achieve a sense of purpose or direction or stability and without them, the future is bleak (see Uya 2012: 792).

F.W. Maitland, (1980:13), a Medieval Historian, adds that: "We study the day before yesterday, in order that yesterday may not paralyse today, and today may not paralyse tomorrow."

Remarks: A greater source of solution to Nigeria's crisis of post-coloniality is for all citizens to arm themselves with history. Of course, if they are not taught the subject formally, they cannot know it and make use of it. Therefore, the history subject should be made compulsory in Secondary schools in Nigeria.

The Imperative of the Teaching of Religious Knowledge in Secondary Schools and Universities in Nigeria

The teaching of Religious Knowledge in Junior Secondary Schools with special emphasis on the three foremost monotheistic religions of African Traditional Religion, Christianity and Islam should be made compulsory. In the Senior Secondary School, the students can take to the study of one religion only. Then in the University system, the current General Studies subject called Peace and Conflict Resolution Studies should be replaced with Nigerian Religions and Peace Education. In this system, the study of the three monotheistic religions should be taught again.

95

Remarks: Most Nigerians are ignorant of the religions of man other than theirs. Besides, few Nigerian Christians have a deeper knowledge of Islam and vice versa, yet there are several areas of inter-penetration and or interface between the two great religions of man. Two of such could be gleaned from the work of Huston Smith (1958:203; 209) thus:

> Islam assumes that the Bibles of the Jews and Christians too were originally authentic revelations from God, which fact entitles those who hold them sacred to be class with Muslims as "People of the Book" ... (Smith 1958:203)

> Islam has a clarity, an order, a precision which is in sharp contrast to the shifting, relative, uncertain, at-sea quality of much of modern life. Muslims explicitly claim this as one of Islam's strengths. God's revelation to man, they say, has proceeded through four great stages. First, through Abraham God revealed the truth of monotheism, God's oneness. Second, through Moses he revealed the Ten Commandments. Third, through Jesus he revealed the Golden Rule, that we love our neighbours as ourselves. All these men were authentic prophets; each nailed down in indispensable planks in the platform of the God-directed life. One question only remained unanswered. How should we love our neighbour? What does the love of neighbour require in this complicated world in which human interests can cross and tangle like pressure hoses on the loose? A final prophet was needed to answer that question and he was Mohammed. Because God answered this final question through him he deserves the title, the Seal of the Prophets. "The glory of Islam consists in having embodied the beautiful sentiment of Jesus into definite laws" (Smith, 1958:209).

These quotations from Huston Smith show clearly the elements of inter-penetration which should be employed in Nigeria for peace, security and cooperation.

Indeed, Christianity recognizes the existence of other religions. In John Gospel 10:16 it is stated: "And the other sheep I have, which are not of this fold: them also I must bring, and they shall hear my voice; and there shall be one fold, and one shepherd". This verse is interpreted to mean diversity in the sight of God and the fact that at the appointed time, all would belong to the same source with God.

The issue of diversity is further underlined by Huston Smith (1958:221) with regards to Islam, another great religion of man. According to him:

The crucial verses in the Koran bearing on the point in question read as follows:

> Let there be no compulsion in religion (ii: 257).

> To everyone have we given a law and a way ... And if God had pleased, he would have made you all (all mankind) one people (people of one religion). But He hath done otherwise, that He might try you in that which He hath severally given unto you: therefore press forward in good works. Unto God shall ye return, and He will tell you that concerning which ye disagree (v: 48).

> Unto you your religion, and unto me my religion (cix: 6) (see Smith, 1958:221).

Nigeria, it should be noted, is a unique country which does not have religious dominance by any religion of man unlike other countries that have either Christians or Muslims as majorities or minorities. What is more, adherents of these different religions number in millions in the country. Indeed, there is no country on earth like Nigeria, which has two major religions in which adherents of each are in excess of 50 million people. Therefore, the citizens should be well-informed about other religions other than theirs that are practised in Nigeria and a deeper understanding of these religions would make them to recoil from offending the sensibilities of adherents of different religions. Lack of knowledge of Christianity and Islam especially by Nigerians is heavily implicated in the crisis of post-coloniality in Nigeria, especially in Northern Nigeria. For these reasons, religious education should be taught in Nigerian Schools and Higher Institutions of learning.

Commencement of the Development of New Cities in Nigeria

As soon as practicable, 50 percent of proceeds from the Excess Crude Account should be used for the development of new cities in Nigeria.

The best antidote to the phenomenon of Boko Haram in Nigeria is economic development. While deliberate efforts should be made to develop agriculture, manufacturing and tourism to generate employment opportunities, the best and urgent approach to the socio-economic and indeed political development of Nigeria is to use the bulk of revenue from crude oil or Associated Gas to fund the development of new cities in each state of the federation. Little Abujas and Lagos should be replicated in all the states of Nigeria where one Senatorial District per state outside the state capital is deliberately developed as a modern-city. Cities, as modern-urban centres, are agents of development.

Urbanization has been successfully used by the developed countries to implement such national goals as: eradicating absolute poverty, maximizing job creation, reducing population growth, reorganizing available economic opportunities and allowing processes of economic development and change from the cities to permeate the entire country (Lawal, 2003:110). Put differently, urbanization is a credible agent of development if properly harnessed. Instead of creating new states and LGCs, the following new cities should be developed in Nigeria:

States	Cities
Abia	Enyimba
Adamawa	Gongola
Akwa Ibom	Atlantic
Anambra	Nnewi
Bauchi	Tafawa Balewa
Bayelsa	Akassa
Benue	Oturkpo
Borno	Kanem Borno
Cross River	Paradise
Delta	Sapele
Ebonyi	Afikpo
Edo	Auchi
Ekiti	Ado
Enugu	Obollo
Gombe	Dukku-Nafada
Imo	Orlu
Jigawa	Hadeja

Kaduna	Nok
Kano	Dalla
Katsina	Funtua
Kebbi	Argungu
Kogi	Confluence
Kwara	Baruten
Lagos	Badagary
Nassarawa	Akwanga
Niger	Kontagora
Ogun	Ijebu
Ondo	Sunshine
Osun	Oduduwa
Oyo	Iseyin
Plateau	Temperate
Rivers*	Oil Rivers; Treasure
Sokoto	Caliphate
Taraba	Mambilla
Yobe	Nguru
Zamfara	Gobir

* Nigeria should develop an oil city in the Niger Delta region as a gift to the region for its oil and the fact that it bears the burden of the political economy of the country for decades; just as South Africa developed the region it mines gold into a Gold City. The most central state in the Niger Delta is Rivers State. Therefore, the Senatorial District in which Ogoniland is located should be developed as Oil Rivers City, whereas the Senatorial District in which Port Harcourt, the State Capital, is not located should be developed as Treasure City.

Each of the new cities would have the capacity to generate a minimum of $1 billion a year and employ a minimum of 100,000 people annually. They would also act as nectars of investment that would magnetize clean and dirty monies, the world over, into their orbits. This implies rapid economic development for Nigeria and the asphyxiation of an unwanted phenomenon like the Boko Haram experience in the country. Besides, the nature of modern cities is that they are designed as security temples and bomb-proofs enclaves.

Normally, a modern city should have, among other things, stadia, Universities, Polytechnics, International Markets, Airports, Airstrips, Residential Areas, International Business Districts, Greenery Parks, Recreational and Security Systems.

Under normal circumstances, it takes a period between a decade and a generation to build a modern city. This being the case, the building plan may start with a Local Government Area or FDD within a Senatorial District and incrementally cover up the rest of the Senatorial District between the first year of its development and twenty five years thereafter.

In terms of funding, it may be necessary for the state governments to fund cities' development by 50 per cent, while the GoN should equally provide the remaining fifty per cent.

In the alternative, monies from Excess Crude Account should be used exclusively for the development of cities in Nigeria. In the plan, one of the three Senatorial Districts outside the one that hosts the capital cities of States should be turned into little Abujas.

Remarks: The development of new cities in Nigeria will create jobs in millions, investment and commercial opportunities and active peace.

Cities are generators of wealth and foreign exchange, especially through urban tourism and international investment.

Tax Evasion

From January 2014, all citizens from the age of 18 years should pay tax and tax evasion should be a treasonable offence.

If the GON implements the short-term and medium strategies as outlined, it would create millions of job opportunities in Agriculture, Manufacturing, Construction, Tourism, Solid Minerals etc.

Nigerians should be mobilized through expansion of economic opportunities to work and assist in the development of the country through taxation.

Nigeria has a federal tax capacity of N15 trillion and individual states have capacities in excess of 500 billion. These should translate into greater capacities for provision of more public goods and job opportunities.

Remarks: The phenomenon of Boko Haram includes tax evasion. Therefore, tax evaders, are literally speaking members of Boko Haram who should have no place in a transformed Nigeria.

Banking and Cashless Economy

To scorch the phenomenon of Boko Haram in Nigeria, all Nigerians from the age of eighteen years should have bank accounts and by 2020, Nigeria should run a cashless economy.

Remarks: Banking and cashless economy would assist in tracking down deviants and saboteurs.

Re-Visiting of the Minimum Wage Regime

The minimum wage in Nigeria should be fixed at Fifty Thousand Naira for Public and Civil servants but for teachers, military, police and paramilitary services, it should be double the amount. This new labour regime should be exchanged with fuel tax, increase in VAT to West African average and collection of tenement rates by the LGCs.

The LGCs should begin to collect tenement rates. It may be necessary to start with corporate buildings and property whose original owners had died. With regards to inherited property, the inheritors should pay yearly tenement on such property and the rate could be One Thousand Naira per room, regardless of the size. The LGCs by law should seize the property where the inheritors lack the capacity to pay tenement and manage or sell them. Corporate buildings and all storey buildings, regardless of size, should equally pay yearly rates of One Thousand Naira per room; other than that, their buildings should be seized by the LGCs and managed or sold out to those who have the capacities to pay tenement.

The West African average of VAT is 15 percent and in Europe that is already developed, it is 20 percent, but in underdeveloped Nigeria, it is 5 percent. As soon as practicable, Nigeria should implement the West African average in its VAT regime and it should be collected by states and shared with their LGCs; the GON should have no business with VAT either as beneficiary or collector.

States should also be encouraged to collect fuel tax. The amount should be determined by the states but the GON should regulate the tax regime by fixing a ceiling of N50 per source of fuel.

In Nigeria, rich people should be classified and defined as those who own storey buildings, inherit(ed) property and car(s) with capacities above 1.5 litre engine. They should, therefore, pay taxes on these property and facilities to sustain the economy and guarantee their security, welfare and wealth.

Remarks: Where payment of taxation is a norm, citizens should be well paid. The multiple sources of taxation means that at the end of the month, about 90 percent of the citizens' earnings or wage would be used up but if the country is developed with taxes, a higher standard of living would be guaranteed the citizens.

Operation of New Constitution

By late 2013, a new Nigerian Constitution should be approved for use in the governance of Nigeria. That Constitution should underline the independent and autonomous status of the LGCs if Nigeria desires peace.

Remarks: Nigeria needs a new Constitution in order to release the energies of its citizens for higher goals of development.

C. Long-Term Strategy, 2015 and Beyond
Presidential Doctrine of 30/70

Through a Presidential Doctrine, budgets of tiers of government from 2015 should have 30 percent Recurrent Expenditure and 70 percent Capital Expenditure.

A credible option to the doctrine is that; by law revenues from the country's minerals resources (crude oil, gaseous and solid minerals) should be used for capital budgets in all tiers of governments and taxes only should be used for recurrent expenditures.

The Gains of Short Term and Medium Term Strategies should be consolidated from 2015.

Sectors to be securitized at all times in Nigeria are: human rights, human capital, natural capital, income distribution (through appropriate taxation), employment, gender sensitivity, justice, rule of law, sports, investment, Nigeria's diaspora and Africa's leadership. These instruments will consolidate active peace and perfect security that Nigeria always aspires for.

Remarks: The economic (development) opportunities from the short term strategic plan era to the medium term would trigger enough opportunities in the OPS for the tiers of government across Nigeria to downsize their already bloated bureaucracies considerably.

Overall Remarks

As already stated, conflicts and crises should not be feared at all. Individuals and entities like nations should rather use them for development and security.

Following from this and the state of crises in the country, President Goodluck Ebele Jonathan is at the crossroads of Nigerian history. He either seizes the opportunity presented by crises in Nigeria to secure and develop Nigeria or continues to administer through the old methods, thereby stoking up a fire that would begin to burn at the twilight of his presidential tenure.

The President needs a three-year state of emergency in the national security of the country to re-direct the energies of the country and its citizens towards purposeful destination. A state of emergency and clearly developed strategic plans within the period are the conditions that would mobilize the citizens of Nigeria for higher goals. In a typical situation of emergency, especially in security sector, a Sword of Damocles hangs on every head and therefore everybody, including members of Boko Haram, would be forced by the logic of circumstances to toe the line; the transformation line, which would result in strong state capacity. Strong states cannot be menaced successfully by deviants.

Finally, it should be known that when the inhabitants of the Tower of Babels are faced with common enemy or hope, they will learn to speak one language. Therefore, a state of emergency should be proclaimed in Nigeria's national security and then used to make all to speak one language; the language of transformation.

It is worth noting that, socio-political transformation can only be carried out successfully by enlightened despots or benign dictators in authoritarianism, but in a democracy, it can only be carried out through strict adherence to the rule of law. This concerns normal democratic practice. In abnormal situations like those of Nigeria, only strict adherence to the rule of law and a national state of emergency, especially on the security sector can save countries from southward dive.

CHAPTER FOUR

Summary and Conclusion

Nigeria is in a state of war. This calls for an emergency response in addition to new approaches to governance. In this regard, the first thing to do is to know the enemy. Therefore, the government should integrate all sources of information and analysis in order to see the enemy as a whole. Integrated, all-source analysis should also inform and shape strategies to do more in order to strengthen the more the security of the Nigerian state. So far it appears as if the Nigerian state does not know its enemy; if it is informed about it, it is not well-informed. This reflects in the state of response which so far is only one millimetre wide and one centimetre deep.

The enemy of Nigeria is a twisted state of its existence which results in imperial administrations that in turn leads to an imperial overstretch and full imperial decline. It is the environment of imperial decline that throws up social actors all over the nation and Boko Haram is just one of them and certainly not the most deadly. Economic and political saboteurs are the ones whose actions even produce groups like Boko Haram.

In this kind of environment Nigeria should re-create itself instead of walking down the path that leads only to a blind alley. When nations are faced with dare-devil challenges, they retool; Nigeria should follow the same path.

The US experience in the aftermath of the 9/11 episode and the recommendations of its probe panel of the 9/11 intelligence failure are quite germane to the shaping of appropriate strategies to contain and tackle the phenomenon of Boko Haram in Nigeria. Below in Box 1.3 is an excerpt from a part of the Report entitled *An Agenda of Opportunity*. That part analyses the structure of the goodwill that the US needs to invest in the Middle East and arising out of that made two critical recommendations.

Box 1.3: Excerpt of the Report of the Probe Panel on 9/11 in the US

AN AGENDA OF OPPORTUNITY

The United States and its friends can stress educational and economic opportunity. The United Nations has rightly equated "literacy as freedom".

- The international community is moving toward setting a concrete goal – to cut the Middle East region's illiteracy rate in half by 2010, targeting women and girls and supporting programs for adult literacy.
- Unglamorous help is needed to support the basics, such as textbooks that translate more of the world's knowledge into local languages and libraries to house such materials. Education about the outside world, or other cultures, is weak.
- More vocational education is needed, too, in trades and business skills. The Middle East can also benefit from some of the programs to bridge the digital divide and increase internet access that have already been developed for other regions of the world.

Education that teaches tolerance, the dignity and value of each individual, and respect for different beliefs is a key element in any global strategy to eliminate Islamist terrorism.

Recommendation: The U.S. government should offer to join with other nations in generously supporting a new International Youth Opportunity Fund. Funds will be spent directly for building and operating primary and secondary schools in those Muslim states that commit to sensibly investing their own money in public education.

Economic openness is essential. Terrorism is not caused by poverty. Indeed, many terrorists come from relatively well-off families. Yet when people lose hope, when societies break down, when countries fragment, the breeding grounds for terrorism are created. Backward economic policies and repressive political regimes slip into societies that are without hope, where ambition and passions have no constructive outlet.

The policies that support economic development and reform also have political implications. Economic and political liberties tend to be linked. Commerce, especially international commerce, requires ongoing cooperation and compromise, the exchange of ideas across cultures, and the peaceful resolution of differences through negotiation or the rule of law. Economic growth expands the middle class, a constituency for further reform. Successful economies rely on vibrant private sectors, which have an interest in cubing indiscriminate government power. Those who develop the practice of controlling their own economic destiny soon desire a voice in their communities and political societies …

Recommendation: A comprehensive U.S. strategy to counter terrorism should include economic policies that encourage development, more open societies, and opportunities for people to improve the lives of their families and to enhance prospects for their children's future.

Source: *Johnson, L. K & J. J. Wirtz. 2008. Intelligence and National Security: The Secret World of Spies. Oxford: Oxford University Press: 426.*

Though there is no terrorism in Nigeria, much less Islamist terrorism, there is need to open up the political space and the economy to accommodate the citizens who are ever ready to contribute their quotas to the development of Nigeria. It is on account of this that the Author has recommended in the Monograph the establishment of the FDDs, SDDs and SFDs in the country, the use of tax regimes to narrow the gap; nay, the gulf between the rich and the poor, the establishment of Security Stations in all Wards in Nigeria, the expansion of the scope of National Intelligence, the creation of State, Local Government and Establishment police systems in addition to the Federal Police whose designation should be the National Guard, the declaration of crude oil and associated gas as **national commons**, and the creation of the Ministries of Charity Affairs in at least the North East and North West geo-political regions of Nigeria to take care of the myriads of social problems in the regions.

Ultimately, Nigerians may have to recognize the obvious fact that whenever peace is mentioned, at least six key words and elements should be seriously considered as its embodiment and these are: justice, equity, equality, co-operation, security and development; take any word out of the calculation, the concept of peace, both positive and negative, becomes a bastard thing. Therefore, to have peace in Nigeria, the GoN should know the enemy of the country. Boko Haram constitutes one of the effects of the security challenges of Nigeria and not the cause. A transformed Nigeria through strategic thoughts and the creation of alternatives are the silver bullets for overcoming the threatening Armageddon.

At this juncture, we may ask this pertinent question: What is the alternative to the Boko Haram phenomenon in Nigeria? It should be noted that whenever social change is desired for a group, such change must be followed by credible alternatives. Writing about the imperatives of providing alternatives in order to scorch corruption and other such vices in Nigeria, Otoabasi Akpan (2011:259) notes:

> To reverse the trend and win the war on financial crimes, Nigeria must go the way of economic development through diversifi-cation of the economy and not through proselytization and sermonization. Diversification will give Nigerians alternatives and criminalize corruption which is a culture today. A culture is a way of life which ordinarily should be promoted but when a culture is identified as bad, only alternatives with overwhelming characteri-zations can supplant it. Illustrations abound even in Nigeria.

Before Mary Slessor, a Christian Evangelist, started evangelization in the Lower Cross River in the colonial period, the people used to practice an aspect of the culture of killing of twins and their mothers; they were exiled to evil forests to die. The prevailing culture was quite functional and like corruption in today's Nigeria, it served the needs of the society and for centuries it was promoted. Miss Slessor used the principles of provisions of alternatives to consign the evil practices into the dustbin of history. The alternatives she brought were Western education and Christianity. The moral forces and functional character of the alternatives dinosaured the practice and quickened the transition of the Lower Cross into modernity. Thus, functional culture of yesterday became barbaric act today. In fact, in modern Nigeria only a moral idiot with a suicidal mania would wish for a renaissance of the old order. Conversely, most citizens pray and wish for twins, triplets and quadruplets. Social changes in societies come through the instrumentality of alternatives. War on corruption in Nigeria can only be won through the Mary Slessor Approach (MSA).

Therefore, both wars on corruption and the phenomenon of Boko Haram in Nigeria can only be won through availability of alternatives. Taken together, these alternatives mean a re-structuring of Nigeria politically, socially and economically; indeed, the country's eager embrace of a new political economy.

Overall, Nigeria should not fear the series of conflicts and crises that torment its soul but should profit largely from them. Its tormentors and torturers are merely in a conversation with the Nigerian state on the themes of justice, security and development. If they are not talking to the deaf after all, then the state will re-discover itself through their efforts and put forward a comprehensive agenda to promote justice, security and development. These call for a grand strategy that should be fertilized by strategic thoughts.

Appendix A

Frontier States and LGCs in Nigeria

S/NO.	STATES	LGCS
1.	ADAMAWA	Fufure
		Ganye
		Jada
		Madagali
		Maiha
		Michika
		Mubi North
		Mubi South
		Toungo
2.	AKWA IBOM	Eastern Obolo
		Eket
		Esit Eket
		Ibuno
		Ikot Abasi
		Mbo
		Okobo
		Oron
3.	BAYELSA	Akuku-Toru
		Brass
		Nembe
		Ekeremor
		Southern Ijaw
4.	BENUE	Kwande
5.	BORNO	Abadam
		Bama
		Gworza
		Kala/Balge
		Kukawa
		Marte
		Mobbar
		Monguno
6.	CROSS RIVER	Akamkpa
		Akpabuyo
		Bakassi
		Boki
		Etung
		Obanliku
7.	DELTA	Burutu
		Warri North

		Warri South West
8.	JIGAWA	Babura
		Maigatari
		Sule-Tankar-kar
9.	KATSINA	Baure
		Jibia
		Kaita
		Mai'Adua
		Marshi
		Zango
10.	KEBBI	Arewa-Dandi
		Bagudu
		Dandi-Suru
11.	KWARA	Baruten
12.	LAGOS	Badagary
		Ijebu Lekki
		Ojo
13.	NIGER	Borgu
14.	OGUN	Egbado North
		Egbado South
		Imeko-Afon
		Ipokia
		Ogun Waterside
15.	ONDO	Ilaje
16.	OYO	Atigbo
		Iwajowa
		Saki West
		Atigbo
17.	RIVERS	Andoni
		Bonny
		Degema
		Opobo-Nkoro
18.	SOKOTO	Gada
		Gudu
		Illela
		Isa
		Sabon-Berni
		Tangaza
19.	TARABA	Kurmi
		Sadauna
20.	YOBE	Machina
		Yunusari
		Yusufari
21.	ZAMFARA	Zurmi

Appendix B

Seven National Questions in Nigeria in Historical Perspective

Apparently, since the beginning of the twentieth century, Nigeria has had about seven national questions that have been unattended to by the Nigerian state and these have acted as brakes to the country's efforts at development. One question pre-dated independence and the other six occurred in the twentieth century independent Nigeria.

The First National question to confront Nigeria was the Northern question which was on the framework of Lugardism. Lugardism refers to a policy of governance in Nigeria where Frederick Lugard, the High Commissioner of Northern Nigeria and later Governor-General of Nigeria, refused to allow agents of social change to penetrate the North and uplift the social climate of the region thereby causing social imbalance with the South at independence. The agents in question were British and (Southern) Nigerian missionaries and merchants. The immediate effect of erecting barriers against these agents was that there was no educational system of the Western type in the Protectorate for many years. Indeed, there was only one school teaching the form of western education in the whole of Muslim area of the North which incidentally formed three-quarters of the Northern Protectorate. This was the school at Nasarawa near Kano with 320 pupils in 1911. Conversely, within the same period in Southern Nigeria and Christian-dominated areas in the North, there were so many schools teaching western education. The system was largely not corrected when Nigeria was amalgamated. Lugardism was a central factor in delaying the date of independence for Nigeria. Where Nigeria was billed to be the first country in the sub-Saharan Africa to gain independence, social factors rooted in Lugardism prevented her and made Ghana to achieve that feat ahead of her. With an undeveloped human resources the North was very cautious about the timing of the country's independence.

At independence, Nigeria ought to have beamed its searchlight on the North to invest in its educational needs but this was not to be. This did not happen not on account of lack of tradition nor principles to anchor the national necessity but because of selfish and narrow-natured politics. It should be noted that as far back as 1951 the expert Commission on revenue allocation, the Hicks and Phillipson

Commission, had recommended special grant to the North to take care of its social limitations. On the principles and amount, Tekena Tamuno (1980:404) records thus:

> Because of Northern Nigeria's under-equipment in schools, roads, hospitals and the like, the 1951 fiscal commissioners recommended a once-and-for all grant of £4 million to that region.

There is no record to show that the grant was ever offered. As no programme was designed for the North in this direction, Nigeria today reaps whirlwind in that part of the country in form of representational killings and disturbances which are erroneously seen as religious crises. Nigeria may experience religious conflicts on account of its being a multi-religious country but certainly does not experience religious crises. Rather the country experiences socio-economic crisis in the shape of religion. The truth of the matter is that in the North these are cases of representational killings and disturbances where the cultural structure of the Western World like Western education, Christianity, government apparatuses and assets of the nouveau-rich represent structures which must be destroyed. The same can be said of the Niger Delta where the white workers, oil installations and the rich in the society represent structures of oppression. Cases of assassination, kidnapping, hostage taking, oil bunkering and vandalisation of oil installations should be seen as aspects of representational killings and disturbances but certainly not militancy. Militancy is alien to Nigerian culture and Nigerians are not psychopaths and neurotic actors; such cases are prevalent in the Western World and not Africa. The flashes of semblance of militancy in Nigeria are products of perennial state of underdevelopment.

Overall, because the Northern question was not tackled and perhaps is still not confronted, Nigeria moves in fits and starts. In specific terms, the first national question was the Northern question and the subsisting one and perhaps the last is the third phase of the Niger Delta Question. The last question can only be solved adequately with due considerations to the Northern question and herein lies the basis for an inclusive peace plan. In other words, the plan must move from the narrow conception of exclusive rights to incorporate wider conception of inclusive common interests. Arguably, Nigeria would not have experienced myriads of crises if the first question had been taken care of.

The Second National Question to confront Nigeria was the first coup d'état. The coup took place on January, 15 1967 and sacked the political system that the British bequeathed to the country at independence. Background to the coup could be situated in the Nigerian political crises in the First Republic. But political crisis is a necessary outcome of constitutional democracy. Without waiting for the crisis to take its course and to appreciate the extent to which the political actors would manage it the military, acting on misguided notion of national interest, struck. In its aftermath one thing was certain; the military which was a neutral institution for crisis management had lost its virginity ... But perhaps if the crisis was well managed the Third National question would not have emerged. This was assault on Nigerian federalism, a system of government that was adopted at independence after series of painstaking negotiation and years of bargaining by the Nigerian people as represented by their leaders...

The Fourth National Question to beset the country was the character of post-civil war transformation which was based on the famous but inactive 3Rs – Rehabilitation, Reconstruction and Reintegration. The immediate end of the war was one period of opportunity that Nigeria ought to have used to strengthen its unity through effective measures of integration and re-integration. But it was not to be as the Igbo people who needed well coordinated rehabilitation programmes were subjected to hardship and repressive measures. Such measures were reflected in the episodes of abandoned-property and homes where all over Nigeria these assets were seized without proper compensation and regardless of the financial worth of individuals, they were forced to exchange the value of their money (Biafran Pound) with pittance of £20 per person. Thus the character of postwar settlement negated the excellent and time-tested military principles of defeat which conditions the victor not to allow the loser to be completely flattened because he could be of use to him in the future. Arguing in this direction, General J. F. C. Fuller in his book, *The Conduct of War* (1962:13) emphasizes that:

> Throughout the history of war, it is noticeable how frequently enemies and friends change sides in rotation. Therefore, once you have knocked your

enemy out, it is wise to set him on his feet again, because the chances are
that you will need his assistance in the next conflict...

The Fifth National question was the Land Use Decree which was
promulgated in 1978 by the Obasanjo military regime. The Decree
was one Imperialist Act that only an Emperor or King in the Dark
Ages of pre-colonial period would have promulgated and forced on his
subjects and not on citizens in the modern era. The Decree was
characterized by brazen seizure of the citizen's land by the state thus
encroaching on the fundamental and, indeed, economic rights of the
people. As a factor of production, land is an asset and its reward is
always rent. But as the Decree transferred ownership of land to the
state, the owners have always been short-changed whenever the state
is interested in such land. If the land has economic crops or building, it
will be assessed and compensation paid; if it does not have any of
these items, no compensation is paid at all. Even the value of
compensation is calculated by the state without any input from the
owner. This is wrong and it is tantamount to state imperialism and
terrorism ...

The Sixth National question was the 1993 June, 12 political crisis
which almost led to the dismemberment of the country. The June 12
episode was a contrived crisis that revolved around the annulment of
the electoral fortunes of Alhaji Moshood Abiola who convincingly
won the Nigerian Presidential election in 1993 ... Consequent upon
the electoral crisis, the South especially the South West where Abiola
came from took up the gauntlet and fought for him to be declared the
winner and inaugurated as the President. That was not to be until
Nigeria compensated the geo-political region by deliberately zoning
the Nigerian Presidency in 1999 to it...

The third phase of the Niger Delta Question is the Seventh
National question that Nigeria is facing. From all indications, it is an
active crisis with the capacity to cause Nigeria to mark the end of
history; to use Fukuyama's phrase (Fukuyama, 2000) ... What is left
for Nigeria to do is to solve the crisis once and for all and stop playing
the ostrich game...

Fundamentally, all the active and inactive crises that Nigeria has
experienced since the Lugardian era have fused to produce the
Nigerian security questions ... For a start, the GON should address the

nation and apologize to the present generation of Nigerians whose forbears were victims of these national questions.

(Extract from Akpan, O. E. 2011. The Niger Delta Question and the Peace Plan. Ibadan: Spectrum Books Limited: 211 – 222).

Appendix C

Natural Resources Available in States in Nigeria

STATES	NATURAL RESOURCES
Abia	Gold, Lead/Zinc, Limestone, Oil/Gas, Salt
Abuja	Cassiterite, Clay, Dolomite, Gold, Lead/Zinc, Marble, Tentalite
Adamawa	Bentonite, Gypsum, Kaolin, Magnesite, Barytes, Bauxite
Akwa Ibom	Clay, Lead/Zinc, Lignite, Limestone, Oil/Gas, Salt, Uranium
Anambra	Clay, Glass-Sand, Gypsum, Iron-Ore, Lead/Zinc, Lignite, Limestone, Phosphate, Salt
Bauchi	Amethyst (Violet), Gypsum, Lead/Zinc, Uranium
Bayelsa	Clay, Gypsum, Lead/Zinc, Lignite, Limestone, Manganese, Oil/Gas, Uranium
Benue	Barytes, Bauxite, Clay, Coal, Gemstone, Gypsum, Iron-Ore, Lead/Zinc, Limestone, Marble, Salt, Oil/Gas
Borno	Bentonite, Clay, Diatomite, Gypsum, Hydro-carbon, Kaolin, Limestone, Oil/Gas
Cross River	Barytes, Lead/Zinc, Lignite, Limestone, Manganese, Oil/Gas, Salt, Uranium
Delta	Clay, Glass-Sand, Gypsum, Iron-Ore, Kaolin, Lignite, Marble, Oil/Gas
Ebonyi	Gold, Lead/Zinc, Salt
Edo	Bitumen, Clay, Dolomite Phosphate, Glass-Sand, Gold, Gypsum, Iron-Ore, Lignite, Limestone, Marble, Oil/Gas
Ekiti	Feldspar, Granite, Kaolin, Syenites, Tatium
Enugu	Coal, Lead/Zinc, Limestone
Gombe	Gemstone, Gypsum
Imo	Gypsum, Lead/Zinc, Lignite, Limestone, Marcasite, Oil/Gas, Phosphate, Salt
Jigawa	Barytes
Kaduna	Amesthyst, Aqua Marine, Asbestos, Clay, Flouspar, Gemstones, Gold, Graphite, Kaolin, Kyanite, Mica,

	Rock Crystal, Ruby, Sapphire, Silhnite, Surpentinite, Tantalite, Topaz, Tourmaline
Kano	Cassiterite, Copper, Gemstone, Glass-Sand, Lead/Zinc, Pyrochinre, Tantalite
Katsina	Kaolin, Marble, Salt
Kebbi	Gold
Kogi	Coal, Dolomite, Feldspar, Gypsum, Iron-Ore, Kaolin, Marble, Talc, Tantalite, Limestone, Gemstone, Bitumen
Kwara	Cassiterite, Columbite, Feldspar, Gold, Iron-Ore, Marble, Mica, Tantalite.
Lagos	Bitumen, Clay, Glass-Sand, Stan tar, Oil/Gas
Nassarawa	Amethyst (Topaz Garnet), Barytes, Beryl, Acquamarine and Hellodor, Cassiterite, Ilmenite, Chalcopyrite, Clay, Colmbite, Cooking Coal, Dolomite/Marble, Feldspar, Galena, Iron-Ore, Limenite, Limestone, Mica, Salt, Sapphire, Talc, Tantalite, Tourmaline, Quartz, Zireon, Zircon.
Niger	Gold, Lead/Zinc, Talc, Iron-Ore
Ogun	Bitumen, Clay, Feldspar, Gemstone, Kaolin, Limestone, Phosphate
Ondo	Bitumen, Clay, Coal, Dimension Stones, Feldspar, Gemstone, Glass-Sand, Granite, Gypsum, Kaolin, Limestone, Bauxite, Oil/Gas
Osun	Columbite, Gold, Granite, Talc, Tantalite, Tourmarine
Oyo	Aquamarine, Cassiterite, Clay, Dolomite, Gemstone, Gold, Kaolin, Marble, Sillimanite, Talc, Tantalite
Plateau	Barytes, Barites, Bauxite, Bentonite, Bismuth, Cassiterite, Clay, Coal, Emerald, Flouride, Gemstone, Gold, Granite, Dolomite, Iron-Ore, Kaolin, Lead/Zinc, Marble, Molybdenite, Phrochlore, Salt, Tantalite/ Columbite, Tin, Wolfram
Rivers	Clay, Glass-Sand, Lignite, Marble, Oil/Gas
Sokoto	Clay, Flakes, Gold, Granite, Gypsum, Kaolin, Laterite, Limestone, Phosphate, Potash, Silica Sand, Salt
Taraba	Lead/Zinc, Kaolin
Yobe	Soda Ash, Diatomite

117

Zamfara   Coal, Gold

Appendix D

Funding, Operations and Strategic Benefits of Proposed New Security Systems in Nigeria

Security is an expensive business. That is why entities that desire to survive must devote a substantial part of their resources for security purposes. As individuals, monies spent on food, accommodation, and clothing – the famous basic necessities of life – are, indeed, funds spent on security because they constitute the very basis of survival which is the kernel of security.

Funding for security services in the states should be sourced from guns tax, homeland tax and security grants. The private citizens with licence to carry guns should pay tax which amount should be determined by government, but not less than N36,000 annually. With regards to the homeland tax, all vehicles above1.5 litre engine should pay N30,000 annually and the Sport Utility Vehicles (SUVs) should pay N50,000 annually. States should establish Security Commissions where the taxes should be paid into and utilized for security purposes including logistics and, provisions of technological peace infrastructure. Security services need fast-moving vehicles including helicopters, power-bikes, and high-tech communication gadgets.

Security calls for a robust war-chest; not financial handouts. Besides, the police should be the highest paid security outfit in the land. Indeed, the police establishment should be organized with insurance packages and lots of incentives to attract young Nigerians; it should be the best security organization that should ultimately be the envy of all.

Be that as it may, the financial package that is erroneously called *security votes* should henceforth be paid into the accounts of States' Security Commissions for use by the Commissions. In a democracy which harps on transparency and accountability, *security votes* which are unaccounted for but are secretly controlled by the different heads of the tiers of government should no longer be allowed to thrive. Its use should be subjected to public scrutiny. In a democracy, even the IC does not have to be excessively secretive in some aspects of their operations and use of public tax. *Security votes* are typical examples of inoculated corruption, deodorized fraud and immune(d) financial crimes that used to be committed by the military junta whose operations in government were shadowy. It should not be allowed to become part of the democratic practice. Therefore, annually the security votes which should now be called *security grants* should be given to Security Commissions and the minimum amount per state should be N5 billion a year.

It is envisaged that a Security Commission in each state would have a minimum of N10 billion annually from the three major sources of revenue outlined. With sufficient fund, it could make the Wards the epicentre of security activities. Therefore, each Ward in the country should have a *security station* which should accommodate all security agencies in Nigeria and members of the IC. In addition, all security stations should have Public Safety Answering Points (PSAPs) linked to all security stations in Nigeria. If these *stations* in the Wards have modern equipment – transportational, communicational and logistics – there would be no hiding place for deviants in the land. The overwhelming presence of police and security personnel with state of the art equipment and logistics is the talisman that Nigeria needs for perfect physical security. This is indeed a *soaking up technique* towards security.

For the transportational, communicational and logistic needs of the Neighbourhood Police, 50 percent of Fund for the States' Security Commissions should be given to the Local Government Security Commissions which should be established in every LGC to take care of these needs. In addition, each LGC should give the Local Government Security Commission annual security grants which should not be less than N100 million.

While the states should pay the salaries and allowances of State Police, the LGCs should pay the salaries and allowances of the Neighbourhood Police and Road Marshals and direct as well their operational use.

In the alternative, the tiers of government and the establishments that operate police system should devote a minimum of 5 percent of their annual budgets for police operations.

With robust financial resources, the LGC Security Commission can change the vehicles of the Neighbour-hood Police every *odd* year, auction same while in every *even* year power-bikes should be purchased for officers and special technified security vehicles for the police outfit.

120

Overall, it is expected that every *odd* year police vehicles should be changed and the old ones auctioned and every *even* year those of other security outfits within the states should similarly be changed and auctioned (Akpan, 2011). In addition, in the *even* years, highly technified security vehicles should be purchased for the police. Besides, as a principle, all middle-level police and para-military personnel should be given power-bikes and magnetic bullet vests to enhance operational efficiency.

Operations of New Physical Security System in Nigeria

The new physical security system in Nigeria should museum the office of the Inspector General of Police (IGP), which should be taken over by the office of the Director-General of the National Security Council (NSC). The NSC is a creation of the 1999 Constitution (see Section 153), though the office of the Director-General of the NSC is not created at the moment, but should be created. With regards to Police matters, the same section creates the institutions of the Nigeria Police Council and the Police Service Commission. These latter establishments should be merged with the NSC. Members of the NSC should include the Chief of Defence Staff, Ministers of Defence, Internal Affairs or Interior and Foreign Affairs, the National Security Adviser, experts in security and defence matters and Director-Generals of States' Security Council, which should be created. The President should be the Chairman of the NSC, while the Vice President should be the Deputy Chairman.

Constitutionally, the Director-General of the NSC should be made ex-officio member of the EXCOF; just as Security Councils should be created for the state and their Director-Generals be made ex-officio members of the States' Executive Councils. In the LGCs, there should be Directors of the Local Government Security Councils which should be created and who should be ex-officio members of the Councils.

Security demands above all else information and communication and it should be the duties of these Security Chiefs of all tiers to be in close contact with the Chief executives of the tiers of government and their cabinet members.

Outside normal duties of security agents, large-scale operational use of the Police and other para-military agencies should be determined by cabinets of the tiers of government and not their Chief executives acting alone.

The Director-General of the NSC should oversee the operational use of all para-military agencies in the country; namely: National Guards, Coast Guards, Border Guards, Environmental Guards, Air Marshals, Custom Services, Immigration Service, Prison Service, Road Marshals, SSS, State Police and Neighbourhood Police. To do this effectively, the mandates of the National Guards and the SSS should include the Monitoring of the Operations and Evaluation of the Performance of all para-military agencies in the country. In other words, to avoid reckless use of these agencies and to install security checks and balances in the country, some security agencies should be mandated to monitor and evaluate the operations and performance of some security agencies. Ideally, it may also be necessary for the Neighbourhood Police to police the State Police and National Guards within their LGCs; just as the State Police should police the Neighbourhood Police and National Guards within the States and the National Guards and SSS should police all security forces in Nigeria. In the final analysis, all citizens should be tuned and trained to become the police of the Nigerian police (and judicial) system(s) and intelligence personnel of the Nigerian IC.

In the states, the DGs of the state Security Councils should head the state police while the Director of Local Government Security Council should head the Neighbourhood Police.

The Governor of a state should continue to be the Chief Security Officer of the state while the Chairman of the LGC should be the Chief Security Officer of the LGC. Equally, the President of Nigeria should continue to be the Chief Security Officer of the country. But in the final analysis, all these Chief Security Officers of the different tiers of government in Nigeria should work through the offices of the DGs and Directors of Security Councils.

Strategic Benefits

Security is the soul of government and once a nation is secured, it can embark on developmental schemes without hitches. What is more, it would have created strategic opportunities for other nations and international investors to come to its orbit as butterflies and bees go to nectar. In other words, a secured nation is a nectar for international investors, development agencies and partners and different classes of tourists.

With a size of almost 1 million square kilometres, a population of 150 million people, a rich history, seductive sights and heritage, investment opportunities and resourceful people, perfect security can fetch Nigeria about $120 billion annually; about four times the value of the country's oil and gas. The soul-searching question is: why does Nigeria allow oil and gas to destroy her and her people and present her at the same time with terrible insecurity dilemma when there are numerous other sources to tap revenue and development opportunities from? Investment in security is not only investment in the national interest of the country but is also a credible source of revenue. Therefore, massive investment, even in physical security, would yield resources that would neutralize the sources of investment funds and provide the country with lots of financial surpluses for developmental purposes.

Bibliography

Akpan, O. E. 2000. *Regional Leadership: Nigeria and the Challenge of Post-Apartheid South Africa.* Uyo: Sure God Press.

Akpan, O. E. 2003. Tragedy at Midday: Oil and Underdevelopment of Nigeria. In Otoabasi Akpan. ed. *The Art and Science of Politics: Essays in Honour of Alhaji Umar Ghali Na'abba*. Port Harcourt: Footsteps Publications:105 – 125.

Akpan, O. E. 2003. The Rise and Fall of Major World Powers: Lessons for Nigeria in Africa. In Otoabasi Akpan. ed. *The Art and Science of Politics: Essays in Honour of Alhaji Umar Ghali Na'abba*. Port Harcourt: Footsteps Publications:296 – 314.

Akpan, O. E. 2005. The GSM Telecommunications and the Nigerian Economy. *Journal of Economics and Management Studies.* vol.(1): 10 – 17.

Akpan, O. E. 2005. Oasis in a Desert: A Profile of South Africa as an Industrial Economy in Africa. *African Journal of Economy and Society*, Vol 6, (1 & 2):18–37.

Akpan, O. E. 2005. The Future as the Past: Understanding the North and South-South and Getting Nigeria on a Straight Path. Unpublished Paper: 1 – 25.

Akpan, O. E. 2007. *Globalization and Arms Trafficking: The Role of Small Arms and Light Weapons (SALWs) in Conflicts and Crimes in Africa.* Paper Presented at the Historical Monthly Seminar of the Department of History and International Studies, University of Uyo, Uyo, on August 31.

Akpan, O. E. 2010. *An Introduction to the Gulf of Guinea: People, History, Political Economy and Strategic Future.* Calabar: 3ple Star Press.

Akpan, O. E. 2010. *Triangulating the Web: Oil, State Capacity and Nigeria's Quest for Sustained Regional Leadership.* Public Lecture to mark the Golden Jubilee of Nigeria's Independence, University of Uyo, Uyo September 28.

Akpan, O. E. 2011. *The Niger Delta Question and the Peace Plan.* Ibadan: Spectrum Books.

Alao, A. 2007. *Natural Resources and Conflict in Africa: The Tragedy of Endowment.* Rochester: Unversity of Rochester Press.

Almond, G. A., G. B. Powell, R. J. Dalton, and K. Strom. 2008. *Comparative Politics Today: A World View.* New York: Pearson Longman.

Auty, R. M. ed. 2001. *Resource Abundance and Economic Development. UNU/WIDER Studies in Development Economics.* Oxford: Oxford University Press.

Ayad, N. 2006. ed. **The Impact of Technology on Intelligence and Security**. London: University of Westminster.

Aydin, A. 2010. Where Do States Go? Strategy in Civil War Intervention. *Journal of the Peace Science Society.* 27 (1): 47 – 66.

Ayoob, M. 1995. *The Third World Security Predicament.* Boulder: Lynne Rienner.

Bakut, T. B. 2010. Global Threats and Africa's Security: Is Africa Relevant? *Nigerian Journal of International Affairs*, 36(1): 91 – 111.

Beaufre, A. 1965. *Introduction to Strategy.* London: Faber and Faber.

Bennis, A. 2006. Intelligence and National Security: A Brief Historical Perspective. In Ayad Nabil. ed. *The Impact of Technology on Intelligence and Security.* London: University of Westminster Press.

Best, S. G. 2007. The Methods of Conflict Resolution and Transformation. In Best, S. G. ed. *Introduction to Peace and Conflict Studies in West Africa: A Reader.* Ibadan: Spectrum Books Ltd.

Best, S. G. 2007. The Methods of Conflict Resolution and Transformation. In Best, Shedrack G. ed. *Introduction to Peace and Conflict Studies in West Africa.* Ibadan: Spectrum Books: 93 – 115.

Barash, D. P. 1994. *Beloved Enemies.* New York: Prometheus Books.

Barnett, J. 2001. *The Meaning of Environmental Security: Ecological Politics and Policy in the New Security Era.* Zeb Books.

Barnett, J. 2007. Environmental Security. In: Collins, A. ed. *Contemporary Security Studies.* London: Oxford University Press.

Boulding, K. 1962. Conflict and Defence. New York: Harper and Row.

Bowman, L. 1985. The Strategic Importance of South Africa to the United States: An Appraisal and Policy Analysis. In: Aluko, O and T. M. Shaw eds. Southern Africa in the 1980s. London: George Allen and Unwin.

Braithwaite, A. 2010. Resisting Infection: How State Capacity Conditions Conflict Contagion. *Journal of Peace Research* 47 (3): 311 – 319.

Buhaug, H. 2010. Dude, Where's My Conflict? Conflict Management and Peace Science: *Journal of the Peace Science Society* 27(2): 107 – 128.

Burton, J. and F. Dukes. 1990. *Conflict: Practices in Management, Settlement and Resolution.* New York: St. Martin's Press.

Buzan, B. and L. Hansen. 2009. *The Evolution of International Security Studies.* London: Cambridge University Press.

Cameron, F. 2002. *US Foreign Policy After the Cold War: Global Hegemon or Reluctant* Sheriff. London: Routledge.

Coker, C. 2002. *Waging War without Warriors? The Changing Culture of Military Conflict*. Boulder: Lynne Rienner

Collier, P. and A. Hoeffler. 1998. *On the Economic Causes of Civil War.* Oxford Economic Papers 50(4):563 – 573.

Coser, L. A. 1968. *The Functions of Social Conflict.* London: Routledge and Kegan Paul.

Deutsch, M. 1973. *The Resolution of Conflict.* New Haven: Yale University Press.

DeRouen, K. *et al* 2010. Civil War Peace Agreement Implementation and State Capacity. *Journal of Peace Research* 47(3): 333 – 346.

de Soysa, I. and E. Neumayer. 2007. Resource Wealth and the Risk of Civil War Onset: Results from a New Dataset of Natural Resource Rents, 1970 – 1999. *Journal of the Peace Science Society* 24(3): 201 – 218.

de Soysa, I. and H. Fjelde. 2010. Is the Hidden Hand an Iron Fist? Capitalism and Civil Peace, 1970 – 2005. *Journal of Peace Research* 47 (3): 287- 298.

Dorussen, Hand H. Ward. 2010. Trade Networks and the Kantian Peace. *Journal of Peace Research* 47(1): 29 – 42

Dowden, R. 2009. *Africa: Altered States, Ordinary Miracles.* London: Portobello Books Ltd.

Ekoko, A. E. 1990. *The Principles and Practices of Alliance Formation and Nigeria's Defence.* In Ekoko, A. E. and M. A Vogt. eds. **Nigerian Defence Policy: Issues and Problems.** Lagos: Malthouse Press Ltd.

Emmers, R. 2007. Securitization. In: Collins, A. ed. *Contemporary Security Studies.* London: Oxford University Press.

Elbadawi, I. and N. Sambanis. 2000. *How Much War Will We See? Estimating the Incidence of Civil War in 161 Countries.* Washington, DC: World Bank.

Falk, R. 2003. *The Great Terror War.* New York: Olive Branch Press.

Fearon, J. D. 2005. Primary Commodities Export and Civil War. *Journal of Conflict Resolution* 49 (4): 483 – 507.

Felthem, R. G. 1998. **Diplomatic Handbook**. Boston: Martinus Nijhoff Publishers.

Fourie, D. F. S. 1998. *Strategic Studies: A Guide.* University of South Africa.

Fukuyama, F. 1992. *The End of History and the Last Man.* New York: The Free Press.

Fuller, J. F. C. 1962. *The Conduct of War*. London: Eyre & Spohiswoode.

Giraldo, J. and H. Trinkunas. 2007. Transnational Crime. In: Collins, A. ed. *Contemporary Security Studies.* London: Oxford University Press.

Gleditsh, K. S. and A. Ruggeri. 2010. Political Structures, Democracy and Civil War. *Journal of Peace Research* 47(3):299 – 310.

Golstein, J. 1988. *Long Cycles: Prosperity and War in Modern Age.* New Haven, C. T: Yale University Press.

Hauss, C. 2000. *Comparative Politics: Domestic Responses to Global Challenges.* Canada: Wadsworth.

Hendrix, C. S. 2010. Measuring State Capacity: Theoretical and Empirical Implications for the Study of Civil Conflict. *Journal of Peace Research* 49 (3): 273 – 285.

Herman, M. 2008. **Intelligence Power in Peace and War**. London: Cambridge University Press.

Homer-Dixon, T. 1999. *Environmental Scarcity and Violence.* Princeton: Princeton University Press.

Hough, P. 2004. *Understanding Global Security.* London: Routledge.

Huston, S. 1958. *The Religions of Man.* New York: Harper & Row Publishers.

Ikpe, E. 2000. *Europe in the Early Modern Period, 1400 – 1700.* Lagos: Darlington and Sons.

Imbua, D, Akpan, O, Amadi, I and Ochefu, Y.eds. *History, Culture, Diasporas and Nation Building: The Collected works of Okon Edet Uya*. Bethesda: Arbi Press, 2012.

Imobighe, T. 2010. Nigeria's National Security in the 21st Century: Challenges of the Emerging Trends in Terrorism: In: Maduagwu, M. O, Akpuru-Aja, A, Jumare, I.M, and Para-Mallam, J.O. eds. *Nigeria's 50 years of Nation-Building: Stock-Taking and Looking Ahead.* Kuru: NIPSS: 475 – 496.

Jackson, R. 2007. Regime Security. In: Collins, A. ed. *Contemporary Security Studies.* London: Oxford University Press.

Johnson, L. K. and J. J. Wirtz. 2008. ed. **Intelligence and National Security: The Secret World of Spies**. New York: Oxford University Press.

Jones, W. S. 1985. *The Logic of International Relations.* Boston: Little, Brown and Company.

Karl, T. 1997. *The Paradox of Plenty: Oil Booms and Petro-States.* Berkeley: CA: University of California Press.

Kean Commission Report: 9/11 Intelligence Failure. In: Johnson, L.K. and J.J. Wirtz. 2008. *Intelligence and National Security: The Secret World of Spies: An Anthology.* Oxford: Oxford University Press: 417 – 458.

Keay, E. A. and H. Thomas. 1965. *West African Government for Nigerian Students.* London: Hutchinson Educational.

Khan, H. 1960. **On Thermonuclear War**. New Jersey: Princeton University Press.

Khan, H. 1962. **Thinking About the Unthinkable**. New York: Horizon.

Klein, J. P., Garry Goertz and Paul F Diehl. 2008. The Peace Scale: Conceptualizing and Operationalizing Non-Rivalry and Peace Conflict. *Journal of Peace Science Society,* 25:67 – 80.

Kolodziej, E. A. 2005. *Security and International Relations.* Cambridge: Cambridge University Press.

Kuran, T. 2004. *Islam and Mammon: The Economic Predicaments of Islamism.* Princeton: Princeton University Press.

Levite, A. 1987. *Intelligence and Strategic Surprise.* New York: Columbia University Press.

Lujala, P. N. P. Gleditsch, and E. Gilmore. 2005. A Diamond Curse? Civil War and a Lootable Resource. *Journal of Conflict Resolution* 49(4): 538 – 562.

Lujala, P. 2010. The Spoils of Nature: Armed Civil Conflict and Rebel Access to Natural Resources. *Journal of Peace Research* 47(1):15 – 28.

Lutz, B. and J. Lutz. 2007. Terrorism. In: Collins, A. ed. *Contemporary Security Studies.* London: Oxford University Press.

Maoz, Z. 2006. *Defending the Holy Land: A Critical Analysis of Israel's Security and Foreign Policy.* Ann Arbor: University of Michigan Press.

McNamara, R. 1968. *The Essence of Security.* London: Hodder and Stoughton

McWilliams, W. C. 1973. Democracy, Publics and Protest: The Problem of Foreign Policy. In Lanyi, G. A. and W. C. McWilliams. eds. *Crisis and Continuity in World Politics: Readings in International Relations.* Toronto: Random House: 378 – 396.

Midgal, J. 1988. *Strong Societies and Weak States: State-Society Relations and State Capabilities in the Third World.* Princeton: Princeton University Press.

Mikdash, Z. 1986. *Transnational Oil: Issues, Policies and Perspectives.* London: Frances Printer.

Modelski, G. 1987. *Long Cycles in World Politics.* Seattle: University of Washington Press.

Morgenthau, H. 1967. *Politics Among Nations.* edn. New York: Knopf.

Nicolaidis, K. 1996. Prevention Action: Developing a Strategic Framework. In: Rotberg, R.ed. *Vigilance and Vengence: NGOs Preventing Ethnic Conflict in Divided Societies.* Washing DC: Brookings Institution Press.

Perry, M. M. Chase, J. R. Jacob, M. C. Jacob and T. H. Von Laue. 2007. **Western Civilizations: Ideas, Politics and Society.** Boston: Hughton Mifflin Company.

Porter, M. E. 1991. *The Competitive Advantage of Nations.* Dialogue: 2 – 9.

Rasler, K. and W. Thompson. 1983. Global Wars, Public Debts and the Long Cycle. *World Politics,* 35:489 – 516.

Rogers, P. 2007. Peace Studies in: Collins, A. ed. *Contemporary Security Studies.* London: Oxford University Press.

Rourke, J. T. 2008. *International Politics on the World Stage.* Boston, McGraw Hill.

Simmel, G. 1955. *Conflict.* New York: The Free Press.

Singer, D. J. 1962. **Deterrence, Arms Control and Disarmament.** Columbus: Ohio State University Press.

Sha, D. P and I. D. Choji. 2011. The Political Class and the Challenges of Democratic Development in Nigeria. In: Maduagwu, M. O, Akpuru-Aja, A, Jumare, I.M, and Para-Mallam, J.O. eds. *Nigeria's 50 years of Nation-Building: Stock-Taking and Looking Ahead.* Kuru: NIPSS: 159 – 178.

Shearer, I.A. 1994. *Starke's International Law. Singapore:* Butterworths

Skocpol, T. 1985. Bringing the State Back In: *Strategies of Analysis in Current Research.* In: P. B. Evans, D. Rueschemeyer & Skocpol (eds.) *Bringing the State Back In.* New York: Cambridge University Press.

Sobek, D. 2010. Masters of their Domains: The Role of State Capacity in Civil Wars. *Journal of Peace Research* 47 (3): 267 – 271.

Sorenson, D. S. 2008. *An Introduction to the Modern Middle East: History, Religion, Political Economy, Economy.* Westview Press.

Soto, H. 2000. *The Mystery of Capitalism: Why Capitalism Triumphs in the West and Fails Everywhere Else.* New York: Basic Books.

Tidwell, A. 2004. *Conflict Resolved? A Critical Assessment of Conflict Resolution.* London: Continuum.

Todaro, M. P., and S. C. Smith. 2004. *Economic Development.* Singapore. Pearson Education Ltd.

Taylor, S. A. 2007. The Role of Intelligence in National Security. In: Collins, A. ed. *Contemporary Security Studies.* London: Oxford University Press.

Thompson, W. R. 1986. Polarity, Long Cycle and Global Power Warfare. *Journal of Conflict Resolution,* 30:587 – 615.

Weber, M. 1919/1958. Politics as a Vocation. In: H. H. Gerth & C. Wright Mills (trans.) *From Max Weber: Essays in Sociology.* New York: Galaxy (77 – 128).

WCED (World Commission on Environment and Development), 1987. *Our Common Future.* Oxford: Oxford University Press.

Wolfers, A. 1962. *Discord and Collaboration.* Baltimore: Johns Hopkins University Press.

Index

A

Ade-Ajayi, Festus, 95
Akpan, Otoabasi, ii, iii, xi, 18, 23, 27, 32, 36, 38, 43, 44, 59, 69, 77, 88, 90, 92, 107, 115, 121, 124, 128
Akwa Ibom State., 38
Almajiri, 61, 75
Almond, Gabriel A, 15, 22, 125
Armitage, Richard, 85
Association of Local Government of Nigeria, 83

B

Bayelsa State, 80, 81
Borno state, 40, 87
Burton, John, 28, 29, 126
Byzantium diplomacy, 49

C

Calabar, 80, 124
Cameroun, 41, 43
Central Africa, 40, 42
Central African Republic, 40
Chado-Hamitic group,, 41
Code of Conduct Bureau, 55, 56

D

dan Fodio, Usman, x, 22, 59
Data-Mining, 48
Department of State Security, viii, 50
Djibouti, 40
Dowden, Richard, 19, 20, 127

E

Early Warning System, 90, 91
Ethiopia, 30, 40

F

Falk, Richard, 63, 64, 127
False-Paradigm Model, 24
Federal Development Districts, 38, 86
Federal Office for the Protection of the Constitution, 50
Federalism, 15

G

Germany, 22, 30, 50, 54, 73
Ghana, x, 30, 111
Globalization blues, 36
Gold City, 99
Greater Horn, 40, 41

www.ingramcontent.com/pod-product-compliance
Lightning Source LLC
Chambersburg PA
CBHW020708270326
41928CB00005B/319